EDITOR: Maryanne Blacker
FOOD EDITOR: Pamela Clark
■ ■ ■
DESIGNER Robbylee Phelan
■ ■ ■
DEPUTY FOOD EDITOR: Jan Castorina
ASSISTANT FOOD EDITOR: Kathy Snowball
ASSOCIATE FOOD EDITOR: Enid Morrison
SENIOR HOME ECONOMISTS: Alexandra McCowan,
Louise Patniotis, Kathy McGarry
HOME ECONOMISTS: Cynthia Black, Leisel Chen,
Kathy McGarry, Tracey Port, Maggie Quickenden,
Dimitra Stais,
EDITORIAL COORDINATOR: Elizabeth Hooper
KITCHEN ASSISTANT: Amy Wong
■ ■ ■
STYLISTS: Lucy Andrews, Marie-Helene Clauzon,
Carolyn Fienberg, Jane Hann, Rosemary de Santis,
PHOTOGRAPHERS: Kevin Brown, Robert Clark,
Robert Taylor, Jon Waddy
■ ■ ■
HOME LIBRARY STAFF:
ASSISTANT EDITOR: Bridget van Tinteren
ART DIRECTOR: Sue de Guingand
EDITORIAL COORDINATOR: Fiona Lambrou
■ ■ ■
ACP PUBLISHER: Richard Walsh
ACP DEPUTY PUBLISHER: Nick Chan
■ ■ ■

Produced by The Australian Women's Weekly Home Library.
Typeset by ACP Color Graphics Pty Ltd.
Printed by Times Printers Pte. Ltd, Singapore.
Published by ACP Publishing Pty Ltd, 54 Park Street, Sydney.

♦ USA: Distributed for Whitecap Books Ltd by
Graphic Arts Center Publishing, 3019 N.W Yeon,
Portland, OR, 97210. Tel: 503-226-2402. Fax: 530-223-1410.

♦ CANADA: Distributed in Canada by Whitecap
Books Ltd, 1086 West 3rd St,
North Vancouver B.C. V7P 3J6.
Tel: 604-980-9852. Fax: 604-980-8197.

■ ■ ■

Salads
Includes index.
ISBN 1 86396 010 4
■ ■ ■

COVER: Best Caesar Salad, page 108.
OPPOSITE: Pickled Vegetables with
Deep-Fried Bocconcini, page 66.
BACK COVER: Open Herb Ravioli with Shrimp
and Pesto, page 45.
INSIDE BACK COVER: Layered Italian Salad, page 70.

W9-BGB-912

Salads

From over 200 recipes you can choose sensational, fresh salads with flavor influences from around the world. They range from the most basic to the very unusual, and there is something for every occasion from a barbeque to a formal sit-down meal. We've used readily available ingredients, plus lots of crispy leaves; the more unusual ones are pictured in our glossary. And if you're wondering how to choose a salad, why not start with the season? Find out what fresh produce is best at the time, then select a method for serving it from among the delicious recipes featured in our book. Even your own garden can provide lettuce, herbs or tomatoes, or you could think of growing some in pots if you don't have a garden.

Pamela Clark

FOOD EDITOR

MAIN COURSES

Some salads in this section are hearty, some are light, and all are satisfying, delicious and as stylish or as simple as the occasion requires. We've made a tempting range based on beef, lamb, pork and veal, poultry, seafood, eggs and cheese, plus some recipes without meat, giving a choice for everyone. Where suitable, some recipes would be equally good as an appetizer if served in smaller portions; others could double as light lunches and snacks. You'll find the quantities in most recipes are easy to adjust depending on how many people you are serving – and their appetites. Most dressings can be made a day ahead; salads are best made just before serving.

NUTTY BEEF AND ASPARAGUS SALAD

1lb fresh asparagus spears
3 tablespoons olive oil
1½lb sliced boneless beef top
   sirloin steak
5oz snow pea sprouts
1 cup (3½oz) pecans or walnuts

TARRAGON DRESSING
3 tablespoons chopped fresh tarragon
3 tablespoons fresh lemon juice
½ cup olive oil
1 teaspoon honey
1 teaspoon French mustard

Boil, steam or microwave asparagus until just tender; drain, rinse under cold water, drain. Heat oil in skillet, add steak in batches, cook until browned and done as desired; cool. Slice steak thinly. Combine asparagus, steak, sprouts and nuts in bowl; drizzle with tarragon dressing.
Tarragon Dressing: Combine all ingredients in screw-top jar; shake well.
Serves 4.

MEATBALL AND MANGO SALAD

Meatballs suitable to freeze.

2lb ground beef
4 teaspoons chopped fresh cilantro
2 cloves garlic, minced
2 green onions, chopped
¾ cup canned unsweetened
   coconut milk
1 cup (2½oz) fresh bread crumbs
2 cups (4½oz) shredded coconut
2 mangoes
2 green onions, extra

DRESSING
½ cup light olive oil
½ cup cider vinegar
2 small fresh red chili peppers,
   finely chopped
4 teaspoons dark brown sugar
1 tablespoon chopped fresh cilantro

Combine beef, cilantro, garlic, chopped onions, coconut milk and bread crumbs in bowl; mix well. Roll 2 teaspoons of mixture into balls, roll in coconut. Place meatballs in single layer on greased baking sheet. Bake, uncovered, in 375˚F oven about 20 minutes or until cooked through, drain; cool.

Cut 1½ of the mangoes into ½ inch x 2½ inch strips. Reserve remaining mango for dressing. Cut extra onions into 2½ inch thin strips. Combine meatballs, mango strips and extra onion strips in large bowl; drizzle with dressing.
Dressing: Chop reserved mango finely, combine with remaining ingredients in screw-top jar; shake well.
Serves 4.

RIGHT: From back: Nutty Beef and Asparagus Salad, Meatball and Mango Salad.

PASTRAMI WITH ROASTED TOMATO AND ONION SALAD

4 teaspoons olive oil
10 (about ½lb) pearl onions
½lb cherry tomatoes, halved
¼ cup olive oil, extra
4 teaspoons chopped fresh
   lemon thyme
4 teaspoons chopped fresh oregano
4 teaspoons chopped fresh basil
2 cloves garlic, minced
12 drained artichoke hearts
2 cups (10oz) frozen broad
   beans (fava)
2 bunches (about ½lb) arugula
1 radicchio lettuce
1 red oak leaf lettuce
¾lb sliced pastrami

DRESSING
½ teaspoon cracked black
   peppercorns
3 tablespoons fresh lemon juice

Heat oil in skillet, add whole onions, cook, stirring, until browned. Transfer onions to roasting pan, bake, uncovered, in 350°F oven 10 minutes; remove from pan.

Place tomatoes, cut-side-up, in roasting pan, sprinkle with extra oil, herbs and garlic. Bake, uncovered, in 350°F oven about 5 minutes or until tomatoes are warm. Remove tomatoes from pan, reserve oil for dressing.

Cut artichokes into quarters. Pour boiling water over beans in heatproof bowl, drain immediately; peel.

Combine onions, tomatoes, artichokes, beans, arugula, torn lettuce and pastrami on plates; drizzle with dressing.
Dressing: Combine reserved oil mixture with remaining ingredients in screw-top jar; shake well.

Serves 4.

BEEF, BOK CHOY AND BLACK BEAN SALAD

Beef can be marinated a day ahead; store, covered, in refrigerator.

1¼lb piece beef tenderloin steak
3 tablespoons light olive oil
1 lime
2 teaspoons Oriental sesame oil
4 teaspoons light olive oil, extra
3 cloves garlic, minced
1 teaspoon grated fresh gingerroot
1 bunch (about 1¼lb) bok
   choy, chopped
2 teaspoons fresh lime juice
2 teaspoons salted black
   beans, rinsed
2 tablespoons black bean sauce
3 tablespoons raw peanuts

MARINADE
3 tablespoons salted black
   beans, rinsed
¼ cup dry sherry
¼ cup light soy sauce
4 teaspoons honey
1 green onion, chopped
¼ teaspoon sambal oelek
¼ teaspoon five-spice powder
1 teaspoon grated fresh gingerroot

Pour marinade over beef in bowl, cover, refrigerate several hours or overnight.

Remove beef from marinade; reserve marinade. Heat oil in skillet, add beef, cook over high heat until well browned all over. Transfer beef to roasting pan, bake, uncovered, in 450°F oven about 10 minutes or until cooked as desired, brushing occasionally with reserved marinade. Stand beef 5 minutes before slicing.

Using a vegetable peeler, cut peel from lime; cut peel into thin strips.

Heat sesame oil and extra oil in wok, add garlic and gingerroot, stir-fry until aromatic. Add bok choy, stir-fry 2 minutes. Add peel, juice, black beans, sauce and peanuts, stir-fry until combined.

Place bok choy mixture on plate, top with sliced beef. Serve warm or cold.
Marinade: Blend or process black beans and sherry until smooth, add remaining ingredients, blend until combined.

Serves 4.

ITALIAN MEATBALL SALAD WITH PESTO WEDGES

Meatballs suitable to freeze.

2 pita pocket breads
⅓ cup mayonnaise
4 teaspoons milk
1 cup (7½oz) orzo pasta
3 tablespoons olive oil
4 teaspoons fresh lemon juice
¼ cup shredded fresh basil
3 tablespoons chopped fresh chives
⅔ cup drained sun-dried
   tomatoes, sliced
5oz mozzarella cheese, chopped
1 cup (5oz) pimiento-stuffed green
   olives, halved

PESTO
1 cup firmly packed fresh basil leaves
1 clove garlic, minced
3 tablespoons pine nuts, toasted
½ cup olive oil

MEATBALLS
1lb ground beef
1 cup (2½oz) fresh bread crumbs
2 cloves garlic, minced
1 onion, grated
1 egg, lightly beaten
oil for deep-frying

Split pita breads in half, cut into wedges. Brush half the pesto mixture onto split side of bread. Place bread, split-side-up, on baking sheet. Bake in 350°F oven about 15 minutes or until bread is crisp; cool.

Combine remaining pesto mixture, mayonnaise and milk in bowl; mix well.

Add pasta to pan of boiling water, boil, uncovered, until just tender; drain, rinse under cold water, drain well. Combine pasta, oil, juice, herbs, tomatoes, cheese, olives and meatballs in bowl; drizzle with pesto mayonnaise mixture. Serve with pesto wedges.
Pesto: Blend or process all ingredients until smooth.
Meatballs: Combine beef, bread crumbs, garlic, onion and egg in bowl; mix well. Roll 2 level teaspoons of mixture into balls. Deep-fry meatballs in hot oil until browned, drain on absorbent paper; cool.

Serves 4.

LEFT: Clockwise from top left: Beef, Bok Choy and Black Bean Salad, Italian Meatball Salad with Pesto Wedges, Pastrami with Roasted Tomato and Onion Salad.

BEEF WITH EGG AND GREEN ONION SALAD

4 teaspoons light olive oil
3 tablespoons Oriental sesame oil
1 onion, finely chopped
2 small fresh red chili peppers,
    finely chopped
4 cloves garlic, minced
2 teaspoons grated lime zest
1/3 cup raw peanuts, chopped
3 tablespoons dried shrimp
1/2 teaspoon ground cardamom
1/2 teaspoon ground cumin
1lb ground beef
1 tablespoon fish sauce
3 tablespoons fresh lime juice
3 tablespoons chopped
    fresh cilantro

EGG AND GREEN ONION SALAD
2 green onions
2 teaspoons Oriental sesame oil
2 teaspoons sweet sherry
2 teaspoons fish sauce
2 teaspoons fresh lime juice
1/2 teaspoon honey
8 eggs
4 teaspoons grated fresh gingerroot

Heat both oils in skillet, add onion, chili peppers, garlic, zest, peanuts, shrimp and spices, cook, stirring, until onion is soft. Add beef, cook, stirring, until beef is browned. Stir in sauce, juice and cilantro; cool. Serve beef mixture with egg and green onion salad.

Egg and Green Onion Salad: Cut onions into 2 inch thin strips. Combine onions, oil, sherry, sauce, juice and honey in bowl.

Whisk eggs and gingerroot together in another bowl. Pour enough egg mixture to cover base of heated greased omelet pan, cook until lightly browned underneath, turn omelet, brown other side. Repeat with remaining mixture. Finely shred omelets, toss with onion mixture. Serves 4.

BELOW: From left: Beef and Three Bell Pepper Salad, Beef with Egg and Green Onion Salad.

BEEF AND THREE BELL PEPPER SALAD

1¼lb piece beef top sirloin steak
2 teaspoons seasoned pepper
4 teaspoons olive oil
2 green bell peppers
2 red bell peppers
2 yellow bell peppers
3 green onions, sliced
1 small bunch chicory

VINAIGRETTE
¼ cup olive oil
4 teaspoons fresh lemon juice
2 teaspoons white wine vinegar
½ teaspoon sugar
½ teaspoon chopped fresh thyme
1 clove garlic, minced

Sprinkle both sides of steak with seasoned pepper. Heat oil in skillet, add steak, cook until done as desired. Remove steak from skillet; cool.

Cut steak into thin slices. Quarter peppers, remove seeds and membranes. Broil peppers, skin-side-up, until skin blisters and blackens. Peel away skin, cut peppers into thin strips. Combine steak, pepper strips, onions and vinaigrette in bowl; mix well. Serve beef and three bell pepper salad with chicory.

Vinaigrette: Combine all ingredients in screw-top jar; shake well.

Serves 4.

JAPANESE-STYLE BEEF SALAD

3 tablespoons light olive oil
8 (about 2lb) beef tenderloin steaks
½ cup (3½oz) short-grain rice
½ x ½oz package nori seaweed
2 carrots
2 stalks celery
½ large (about 7oz) daikon
4 radishes, coarsely grated
1½oz package pickled pink
    gingerroot, finely shredded

SOY AND SESAME SAUCE
4 teaspoons light soy sauce
4 teaspoons mirin
1 teaspoon sesame seeds
½ teaspoon sugar
¼ teaspoon Oriental sesame oil

WASABI SAUCE
2 teaspoons wasabi paste
4 teaspoons mirin
4 teaspoons water

Heat oil in skillet, add steaks, cook until well browned and done as desired; remove from skillet, cool.

Slice steaks thinly. Add rice gradually to pan of boiling water, boil, uncovered, until tender; drain, rinse under cold water, cool. Spoon rice into 4 molds (½ cup capacity), press down firmly.

Place seaweed in bowl, cover with cold water, stand until softened; drain, pat dry with absorbent paper. Shred seaweed finely.

Cut carrots, celery and daikon into long, thin strips. Place all ingredients separately on individual plates; top rice with seaweed shreds. Serve salad with soy and sesame sauce and wasabi sauce.

Soy and Sesame Sauce: Combine all ingredients in screw-top jar; shake well.

Wasabi Sauce: Blend paste, mirin and water in bowl; mix well.

Serves 4.

ABOVE: Japanese-Style Beef Salad.

BARBEQUED BEEF AND BEET SALAD

6 beets
3 oranges
3 tablespoons chopped fresh tarragon
1 green bell pepper, finely sliced
2 green onions, chopped
2½lb piece beef tenderloin,
    thinly sliced
2 green oak leaf lettuces

DRESSING
1 cup fresh orange juice
2 tablespoons tarragon vinegar
2 teaspoons prepared horseradish
¼ teaspoon sugar
3 tablespoons chopped fresh tarragon
1 clove garlic, minced
½ teaspoon French mustard
¾ cup olive oil

Cut leaves from beets, reserve 12 leaves. Grate beets.

Using vegetable peeler, cut peel thinly from oranges, cut peel into thin strips.

Combine beets, peel, tarragon and 1¼ cups of the dressing in bowl, cover, stand 2 hours. Just before serving, add pepper and onions; mix well.

Broil or barbeque beef slices until cooked as desired.

Toss reserved beet leaves and torn lettuce leaves in remaining dressing, top with beet salad and beef.

Dressing: Combine all ingredients in screw-top jar; shake well.

Serves 6.

BEEF AND VEGETABLE SHELLS WITH GINGERROOT DRESSING

Steak can be marinated a day ahead; store, covered, in refrigerator.

1lb boneless beef top sirloin steak,
   thinly sliced
4 teaspoons light olive oil
2 carrots
1 red bell pepper
1 yellow bell pepper
2 zucchini
2 stalks celery
4 teaspoons light olive oil, extra
1 clove garlic, minced
4 teaspoons light soy sauce
20 extra large pasta shells

MARINADE
3 tablespoons light soy sauce
4 teaspoons Oriental sesame oil
4 teaspoons honey
4 teaspoons dark brown sugar
1 teaspoon five-spice powder
2 cloves garlic, minced
4 teaspoons grated fresh gingerroot
3 tablespoons sweet sherry

DRESSING
4 teaspoons soy sauce
3 tablespoons Oriental sesame oil
3 tablespoons dark brown sugar
4 teaspoons grated fresh gingerroot

Combine steak with marinade in bowl, cover, refrigerate several hours or overnight. Drain steak from marinade, discard marinade. Heat oil in skillet, cook steak in batches until well browned and cooked; drain on absorbent paper.

Cut carrots, peppers, zucchini and celery into thin strips. Heat extra oil in skillet, add vegetables and garlic, stir-fry until just tender, stir in sauce; cool. Combine steak and vegetable mixture in bowl.

Add pasta to large pan of boiling water, boil, uncovered, until just tender; drain. Spoon the steak and vegetable mixture into each pasta shell; drizzle with dressing.
Marinade: Combine all ingredients in bowl; mix well.
Dressing: Combine all ingredients in screw-top jar; shake well.
Serves 4.

RED CABBAGE, SAUSAGE AND CILANTRO SALAD

8 (about 1½lb) thick beef sausages
½lb spaghetti pasta
½ small red cabbage, shredded
8 green onions, chopped
12 fresh dates, pitted, sliced

DRESSING
⅓ cup chopped fresh cilantro
4 teaspoons chopped fresh basil
4 teaspoons grated Parmesan cheese
⅓ cup olive oil
3 tablespoons fresh lime juice
1 clove garlic, minced
½ teaspoon sambal oelek

Cook sausages in skillet until browned and cooked through; drain on absorbent paper, cool. Slice sausages thinly.

Add pasta to large pan of boiling water, boil, uncovered, until just tender; drain, rinse under cold water, drain well.

Combine sausages, pasta, cabbage, onions, dates and dressing in bowl, cover, refrigerate 1 hour.
Dressing: Blend or process all ingredients until smooth.
Serves 4.

HOT STEAK AND CRUNCHY POTATO SALAD

1¼lb beef tenderloin steak
2 teaspoons seasoned pepper
2 teaspoons garlic salt
4 teaspoons light olive oil
1 romaine lettuce
1 bunch (about 1¼lb) spinach,
   shredded
2 cups (about 3½oz) firmly packed
   watercress sprigs
2 small avocados, sliced

CRUNCHY POTATOES
2 potatoes
4 teaspoons light olive oil
1 tablespoon butter

CREAMY DRESSING
2 teaspoons seeded mustard
2 teaspoons horseradish cream
1 teaspoon dark brown sugar
⅓ cup olive oil
2 tablespoons white wine vinegar
⅓ cup heavy cream

Cut steak evenly into ½ inch strips. Combine steak, pepper and salt in bowl. Heat oil in skillet, add steak, cook in batches until browned and cooked as desired; drain on absorbent paper.

Combine torn lettuce leaves, spinach and watercress in bowl, top with avocados, hot steak and crunchy potatoes; drizzle with creamy dressing.
Crunchy Potatoes: Peel potatoes, cut into ½ inch cubes. Heat oil and butter in roasting pan, add potatoes, stir to coat in oil mixture. Bake, in 400°F oven about 35 minutes or until crisp, turning occasionally; drain well on absorbent paper.
Creamy Dressing: Combine all ingredients in pan, whisk over heat until warm.
Serves 4.

LEFT: Clockwise from back: Red Cabbage, Sausage and Cilantro Salad, Beef and Vegetable Shells with Gingerroot Dressing, Barbequed Beef and Beet Salad.
ABOVE: Hot Steak and Crunchy Potato Salad.

BEEF AND BEAN SALAD WITH BELL PEPPER MAYONNAISE

2½lb boneless beef sirloin
4 teaspoons olive oil
½lb long beans
½lb cherry tomatoes
½lb mini yellow pear tomatoes
1 cup (about 6oz) small black olives
⅓ cup shredded fresh basil
3 tablespoons chopped fresh chives
3 tablespoons chopped fresh parsley

DRESSING
1 clove garlic, minced
2 tablespoons balsamic vinegar
½ cup virgin olive oil

BELL PEPPER MAYONNAISE
1 large red bell pepper
1 egg yolk
½ teaspoon French mustard
1 teaspoon white wine vinegar
¼ cup olive oil
¼ cup grapeseed oil

Tie beef with kitchen string at 1½ inch intervals. Heat oil in skillet, add beef, cook until well browned all over. Transfer beef to wire rack in roasting pan, bake, uncovered, in 375°F oven about 25 minutes or until cooked as desired; cool.

Cut beans into 4 inch lengths. Boil, steam or microwave beans until just tender; drain, rinse under cold water, drain. Combine beans, tomatoes, olives, herbs and dressing in bowl; mix well. Serve bean salad with sliced beef and bell pepper mayonnaise.

Dressing: Combine all ingredients in screw-top jar; shake well.

Bell Pepper Mayonnaise: Quarter pepper, remove seeds and membrane. Broil pepper, skin-side-up, until skin blisters and blackens; peel skin. Blend or process pepper until smooth, push through sieve. Blend or process egg yolk, mustard and vinegar until smooth. With motor operating, gradually pour in combined oils in a thin stream, blend until thickened. Add pepper puree, blend until smooth.

Serves 6.

THAI-STYLE BEEF SALAD

1 red bell pepper
4 teaspoons light olive oil
1¼lb piece beef top sirloin steak
1oz rice vermicelli noodles
oil for deep-frying
1 small romaine lettuce
1 small radicchio lettuce
2 tomatoes, peeled,
    seeded, chopped
2 green onions, chopped

DRESSING
⅓ cup fresh lime juice
¼ cup fish sauce
4 teaspoons chopped fresh
    lemon grass
4 teaspoons chopped fresh mint
4 teaspoons chopped fresh cilantro
4 teaspoons honey
1 clove garlic, minced
2 small fresh red chili peppers,
    finely chopped

Quarter pepper, remove seeds and membrane. Broil pepper, skin-side-up, until skin blisters and blackens. Peel skin, cut pepper into strips. Heat oil in skillet, add steak, cook until well browned and done as desired. Remove steak from skillet; cool.

Cut steak into thin slices. Combine steak and 3 tablespoons of the dressing in bowl; mix well.

Deep-fry noodles in batches in hot oil about 5 seconds or until puffed and white; drain on absorbent paper.

Combine pepper, torn lettuce leaves, tomatoes, onions and remaining dressing in bowl. Place lettuce mixture on plates, top mixture with steak then crisp noodles.
Dressing: Combine all ingredients in screw-top jar; shake well.

Serves 4.

BEEF SALAD CUPS WITH TOMATO SALSA

4 teaspoons light olive oil
2 large onions, finely chopped
1lb ground beef
2 cloves garlic, minced
1 teaspoon beef instant bouillon
1 Belgian endive
¼ cup Parmesan cheese flakes

TOMATO SALSA
½lb cherry tomatoes, quartered
6 green onions, chopped
3 tablespoons olive oil
4 teaspoons fresh lemon juice

Heat oil in skillet, add onions, cook, stirring, until soft, add beef, garlic and instant bouillon, cook, stirring, until beef is browned and mixture dry. Transfer to bowl, cool.

Cover beef mixture, refrigerate until cold. Separate endive leaves. Spoon beef mixture into leaves, serve topped with tomato salsa and cheese.
Tomato Salsa: Combine all ingredients in bowl; cover, refrigerate 1 hour.
Serves 4.

ABOVE: Thai-Style Beef Salad.
RIGHT: From left: Beef and Bean Salad with Bell Pepper Mayonnaise, Beef Salad Cups with Tomato Salsa.

CREAMY LAMB AND SWISS CHEESE SALAD

4 teaspoons light olive oil
1¼lb lamb leg center slices
7oz Swiss cheese, sliced
10 dill pickles, sliced
½lb cherry tomatoes, halved
4 green onions, chopped
6 romaine lettuce leaves
6 Boston lettuce leaves

DRESSING
2 teaspoons chopped fresh dill
1 cup light sour cream
4 teaspoons seeded mustard
4 teaspoons horseradish cream
4 teaspoons cracked black
peppercorns

Heat oil in skillet, add lamb, cook until browned and cooked as desired; drain, cool. Cut lamb into thin strips. Cut cheese into thin strips. Combine lamb, cheese, pickles, tomatoes, onions and torn lettuce leaves in bowl, add dressing; mix well.
Dressing: Combine all ingredients in bowl; mix well.

Serves 4 to 6.

LAMB FILLET SALAD WITH SPICED GARBANZO BEANS

Garbanzo beans are best prepared a day ahead; keep, covered, at room temperature. If you prefer, use 2 x 8¾oz cans garbanzo beans; drain and rinse before using.

1 cup (7oz) dried garbanzo beans
1 teaspoon ground cumin
1 teaspoon ground coriander
4 teaspoons curry powder
¼ teaspoon chili powder
3 tablespoons light olive oil
4 teaspoons light olive oil, extra
6 (about 1lb) lamb fillets

SALAD
1 cup firmly packed flat-leafed
parsley, chopped
⅓ cup chopped fresh mint
1 clove garlic, minced
2 tomatoes, peeled, seeded, chopped
1 small green cucumber, chopped

TOMATO CUMIN DRESSING
2 teaspoons cuminseed
14½oz can tomatoes
¼ cup olive oil
4 teaspoons white vinegar
4 teaspoons balsamic vinegar
1 teaspoon seasoned pepper

Place beans in large bowl, cover well with water, cover, stand overnight.

Drain beans, rinse well. Add beans to pan of boiling water, simmer, uncovered, about 30 minutes or until tender; drain. Toss beans in combined spices and oil, spread in single layer on baking sheet, bake, uncovered, in 375°F oven about 45 minutes or until beans are lightly browned and crisp.

Heat extra oil in pan, add lamb in batches, cook until tender; drain, cool. Slice lamb thinly. Top salad with garbanzo beans and lamb; drizzle with tomato cumin dressing.
Salad: Combine all ingredients in bowl; mix well.
Tomato Cumin Dressing: Add cuminseed to dry pan, stir over heat until fragrant. Blend or process undrained tomatoes until smooth; strain, discard tomato seeds. Combine cuminseed, strained puree, oil, both vinegars and pepper in screw-top jar; shake well.

Serves 4.

BARBEQUED LAMB CHOPS WITH POLENTA

12 Frenched lamb rib chops
1 large radicchio lettuce
1 large fennel bulb, thinly sliced
½ cup drained sun-dried
tomatoes, sliced
½ cup black olives, pitted, sliced
½ cup shredded fresh basil
1 cup firmly packed flat-leafed parsley
½ cup Parmesan cheese flakes

DRESSING
3 tablespoons balsamic vinegar
2 cloves garlic, minced
4 teaspoons tomato paste
4 teaspoons water
⅔ cup virgin olive oil

POLENTA
2½ cups chicken broth
1½ cups (½lb) yellow cornmeal
¼ cup grated Parmesan cheese
1 egg yolk
4 teaspoons chopped fresh rosemary
oil for deep-frying

Barbeque or broil lamb until cooked as desired. Combine lettuce leaves, fennel, tomatoes, olives, basil, parsley and cheese in bowl, add half the dressing; mix gently. Drizzle lamb with remaining dressing; serve with salad and polenta.
Dressing: Combine all ingredients in screw-top jar; shake well.
Polenta: Grease 3 inch x 10½ inch baking pan, line base with baking paper, grease paper. Place broth in pan, bring to boil, add cornmeal, cook, stirring, about 7 minutes or until mixture is thick; cool 3 minutes. Stir in cheese, egg yolk and rosemary. Press mixture into prepared pan, cover, refrigerate 2 hours. Turn polenta out of pan, cut into 16 triangles. Deep-fry polenta in hot oil until browned; drain on absorbent paper.

Serves 4 to 6.

LEFT: Clockwise from top left: Barbequed Lamb Chops with Polenta, Creamy Lamb and Swiss Cheese Salad, Lamb Fillet Salad with Spiced Garbanzo Beans.

LAMB FILLET SALAD WITH WILD RICE

Lamb can be marinated a day ahead; store, covered, in refrigerator.

4 (about ¾lb) lamb fillets
4 teaspoons light olive oil
1 small onion, grated
1 small fresh green chili pepper, finely chopped
1 clove garlic, minced
1 teaspoon white wine vinegar
4 teaspoons teriyaki sauce
4 teaspoons honey
⅔ cup wild rice
½lb sweet potato
1lb green beans

DRESSING
½ x 10oz package frozen spinach, thawed
3 tablespoons chopped fresh cilantro
4 teaspoons fresh lime juice
½ teaspoon Oriental sesame oil
2 teaspoons fish sauce
⅓ cup buttermilk
¼ teaspoon sugar
¼ cup water

Combine lamb, oil, onion, chili pepper, garlic, vinegar, sauce and honey in bowl, cover, refrigerate several hours or overnight.

Remove lamb from marinade, reserve marinade. Place lamb in roasting pan, bake, uncovered, in 400°F oven about 10 minutes or until cooked as desired, brushing occasionally with reserved marinade. Cool lamb, slice thinly.

Add rice to pan of boiling water, boil, uncovered, about 40 minutes or until tender, drain.

Cut sweet potato into ½ inch pieces. Cut beans into 2 inch lengths. Boil, steam or microwave sweet potato and beans separately until tender; drain, rinse under cold water, drain well. Place rice, sweet potato, beans and lamb on plates; drizzle with dressing.

Dressing: Blend or process all ingredients until smooth, push through fine sieve; cover, refrigerate 30 minutes.

Serves 4.

TANDOORI LAMB WITH PINEAPPLE SALSA

Lamb can be marinated a day ahead; store, covered, in refrigerator. Marinated lamb suitable to freeze.

12 Frenched lamb rib chops
2 cups plain yogurt
6 cloves garlic, minced
2 tablespoons grated fresh gingerroot
2 tablespoons paprika
1 teaspoon garam masala
⅛ teaspoon ground saffron
1½ teaspoons ground cardamom
½ teaspoon chili powder
1 teaspoon ground coriander
1 teaspoon grated lemon zest
3 tablespoons fresh lime juice

PINEAPPLE SALSA
½ small pineapple, finely chopped
1 small green cucumber, finely chopped
2 teaspoons chopped fresh cilantro
4 teaspoons fresh lime juice

Place lamb in large bowl, pour over combined remaining ingredients, cover, refrigerate several hours or overnight.

Remove lamb from marinade, reserve marinade. Broil or barbeque lamb until cooked as desired, brushing with reserved marinade during cooking; cool. Serve tandoori lamb with pineapple salsa.

Pineapple Salsa: Combine all ingredients in bowl; cover, stand 1 hour.

Serves 4.

ABOVE LEFT: Tandoori Lamb with Pineapple Salsa.
RIGHT: From back: Lamb Fillet Salad with Wild Rice, Herbed Lamb Sausages with Rosemary Pasta.

HERBED LAMB SAUSAGES WITH ROSEMARY PASTA

2 cups all-purpose flour
¼ cup chopped fresh rosemary
3 eggs
1 red bell pepper, thinly sliced

GARLIC DRESSING
2 egg yolks
3 tablespoons white wine vinegar
3 cloves garlic, minced
2 teaspoons Dijon mustard
1⅓ cups salad oil
3 tablespoons water

HERBED LAMB SAUSAGES
2lb shoulder of lamb, boned
2 tablespoons (¼ stick) butter
1 onion, finely chopped
2 teaspoons sambal oelek
2 cloves garlic, minced
1 egg
1 cup (2½oz) fresh bread crumbs
3 tablespoons chopped fresh parsley
4 teaspoons chopped fresh thyme
2 teaspoons olive oil

Mix flour, rosemary and eggs in bowl or processor until mixture forms a ball, adding a little water, if necessary (mixture should be firm but not flaky). Knead dough on lightly floured surface until smooth.

If making pasta by hand, cover dough, stand 20 minutes. Roll on lightly floured surface until about 1⁄16 inch thick.

If using pasta machine, cut dough in half, roll each half through thickest setting of machine, fold dough in half. Repeat rolling and folding dough, gradually decreasing setting on machine until dough is about 1⁄16 inch thick.

Cut pasta into ¾ inch strips. Add pasta to large pan of boiling water, boil, uncovered, about 5 minutes or until just tender; drain, rinse under cold water, drain. Combine pasta, pepper, garlic dressing and herbed lamb sausages in bowl; mix gently.

Garlic Dressing: Place egg yolks, vinegar, garlic and mustard in bowl, whisk until smooth. Add oil gradually in a thin stream while whisking, whisk until thick; stir in water.

Herbed Lamb Sausages: Trim fat from lamb, chop lamb roughly. Heat butter in skillet, add onion, sambal oelek and garlic, cook, stirring, until onion is soft, cool. Process lamb, onion mixture and egg until smooth. Transfer mixture to bowl, stir in bread crumbs and herbs. Divide mixture into 4 portions.

Spoon 1 portion of mixture along center of piece of plastic wrap. Fold plastic wrap around mixture, forming sausage shape about 1¼ inches in diameter. Repeat with remaining mixture. Wrap each roll in foil, twist ends to seal.

Add rolls to large pan of simmering water, simmer, covered, 10 minutes. Remove rolls from water, stand 5 minutes before unwrapping. Heat oil skillet, add sausages, cook until lightly browned all over; drain on absorbent paper; cool. Cut sausages diagonally into thin slices.

Serves 6.

BAKED LAMB AND EGGPLANT WITH GARLIC MAYONNAISE

3lb leg of lamb
1 large egglant
coarse (kosher) salt
¼ cup olive oil
1 bunch (about 1¼lb) spinach,
    shredded
½ cup black olives, pitted, quartered
6oz feta cheese, cubed
¼ cup pine nuts, toasted

GARLIC MAYONNAISE
1 egg yolk
1 whole egg
1 clove garlic, minced
1 teaspoon Dijon mustard
3 tablespoons fresh lemon juice
1 cup salad oil
4 teaspoons chopped fresh parsley

Place lamb on wire rack in roasting pan, bake, uncovered, in 350°F oven about 1½ hours or until cooked as desired; cool.

Cut eggplant into ½ inch cubes, sprinkle with salt, stand 20 minutes. Rinse eggplant under cold water, drain, pat dry with absorbent paper. Place eggplant in single layer in roasting pan, drizzle evenly with oil. Bake, uncovered, in 350°F oven about 30 minutes or until just tender, stirring occasionally; cool. Top spinach with sliced lamb, eggplant, olives, cheese and pine nuts; serve with garlic mayonnaise.
Garlic Mayonnaise: Combine egg yolk, egg, garlic, mustard and half the juice in blender, blend 1 minute.

With motor operating, add half the oil in a slow steady stream. Add remaining juice then continue pouring oil in a thin stream; blend until thick. Transfer mayonnaise to bowl; stir in parsley.

Serves 6.

MARINATED LAMB WITH NUTTY CITRUS SALAD

Lamb is best marinated a day ahead; store, covered, in refrigerator.

4 teaspoons olive oil
6 (about 1lb) lamb fillets
¼ cup fresh orange juice
¼ cup fresh lemon juice
4 teaspoons balsamic vinegar
½ cup olive oil, extra
1 teaspoon grated lemon zest
1 lollo rosso lettuce
4 oranges, segmented
2 grapefuit, segmented
⅔ cup blanched whole almonds,
    toasted
4 green onions, chopped
1½ cups (about 2½oz) firmly packed
    watercress sprigs

Heat oil in skillet, add lamb in batches, cook until browned or cooked as desired, drain on absorbent paper.

Slice lamb. Combine lamb, juices, vinegar, extra oil and zest in bowl; cover, refrigerate several hours or overnight.

Drain lamb, reserve marinade. Combine lamb, torn lettuce leaves, citrus segments, nuts, onions and watercress in bowl; drizzle with reserved marinade.

Serves 4.

LAMB AND POTATO SALAD WITH MINT DRESSING

2lb baby new potatoes
3 tablespoons olive oil
10 (about 1¾lb) lamb fillets
3 tablespoons chopped fresh chives

MINT DRESSING
4 egg yolks
⅓ cup fresh lime juice
2 cloves garlic, minced
¼ cup grapeseed oil
½ cup salad oil
1 cup chopped fresh mint

Boil, steam or microwave potatoes until tender; drain.

Heat oil in skillet, add lamb in batches, cook until well browned or cooked as desired; drain on absorbent paper.

Slice lamb. Combine potatoes and lamb in bowl, add dressing; mix gently, sprinkle with chives. Serve warm or cold.
Mint Dressing: Blend or process egg yolks, juice and garlic until smooth. Add combined oils gradually in a thin stream while motor is operating. Add mint, blend until combined.

Serves 6.

LEFT: Baked Lamb and Eggplant with Garlic Mayonnaise.
RIGHT: From left: Lamb and Potato Salad with Mint Dressing, Marinated Lamb with Nutty Citrus Salad.

LAMB PROSCIUTTO WITH MARINATED MUSHROOMS

5oz sliced lamb prosciutto
1 radicchio lettuce
½ bunch (about 10oz) spinach
1 cup (about 1½oz) firmly packed
    watercress leaves
½ cup olive oil
3 tablespoons balsamic vinegar
½ cup firmly packed fresh purple
    basil leaves
oil for deep-frying

MARINATED MUSHROOMS
10 dried Chinese mushrooms
2½oz Shitake mushrooms, chopped
5oz oyster mushrooms, halved
10oz button mushrooms, quartered
2 cloves garlic, minced
1 small red onion, finely chopped
1 tablespoon grated lemon zest
3 tablespoons chopped fresh
    rosemary
¼ cup chopped fresh parsley
½ cup fresh lemon juice
1¼ cups olive oil

Cut lamb, lettuce and spinach into thin strips. Combine lamb, lettuce, spinach, watercress, oil and vinegar in bowl; mix well. Deep-fry basil leaves in hot oil about 30 seconds or until crisp. Top lamb mixture with marinated mushrooms, sprinkle with basil leaves.
Marinated Mushrooms: Place dried mushrooms in bowl, cover with boiling water, stand 20 minutes. Drain mushrooms, discard liquid and stems; slice mushrooms thinly. Combine all mushrooms and remaining ingredients in bowl, stand 2 hours, stirring occasionally.

Serves 4.

COUSCOUS TABBOULEH WITH LAMB MEATBALLS

Meatballs suitable to freeze.

1 cup boiling water
1½ cups (½lb) couscous
⅓ cup olive oil
1 clove garlic, minced
2 red bell peppers, finely chopped
1½ cups chopped fresh parsley
8 green onions, chopped
¾ cup grated Parmesan cheese

DRESSING
¼ cup olive oil
4 teaspoons red wine vinegar
4 teaspoons fresh lemon juice

LAMB MEATBALLS
1lb ground lamb
1 large onion, grated
4 teaspoons chopped fresh sage
3 cloves garlic, minced
4 teaspoons tomato paste
1 egg, lightly beaten
1½ cups (3½oz) fresh bread crumbs

Pour water over couscous in bowl, stir, stand until water is absorbed. Heat oil in skillet, add garlic and couscous, cook, stirring, until well combined; cool. Combine couscous mixture, peppers, parsley, onions, cheese and dressing in bowl; mix well. Stir in lamb meatballs.
Dressing: Combine all ingredients in screw-top jar; shake well.
Lamb Meatballs: Combine all ingredients in bowl, mix well, cover, refrigerate 30 minutes. Roll 2 level teaspoons of mixture into balls, place in single layer on lightly greased baking sheet, bake, uncovered, in 400°F oven about 20 minutes or until browned and cooked through; cool.

Serves 4.

RIGHT: Clockwise from back: Couscous Tabbouleh with Lamb Meatballs, Lamb Prosciutto with Marinated Mushrooms, Lemon-Crusted Lamb with Tahini Dip.

LEMON-CRUSTED LAMB WITH TAHINI DIP

3 tablespoons pine nuts
3 tablespoons old-fashioned oats
3 tablespoons sesame seeds
¾ cup packaged unseasoned bread crumbs
1 teaspoon grated lemon zest
2 teaspoons honey
2 teaspoons chopped fresh thyme
3 tablespoons chopped fresh parsley
¼ cup grated Parmesan cheese
1 egg yolk
10 (about 1¾lb) lamb fillets
all-purpose flour
1 egg, lightly beaten
4 teaspoons milk
¼ cup light olive oil
2 lemons
2 limes
2 bunches (about ½lb) arugula
2 cups (about 2½oz) snow pea sprouts

DRESSING
2 tablespoons fresh lemon juice
¼ cup olive oil

TAHINI DIP
⅓ cup plain yogurt
4 teaspoons fresh lemon juice
2 tablespoons tahini (sesame paste)

Process nuts, oats and sesame seeds until smooth; transfer mixture to bowl. Stir in bread crumbs, zest, honey, herbs, cheese and egg yolk; mix well. Toss lamb in flour, shake away excess flour. Dip lamb into combined egg and milk, toss in bread crumb mixture, press bread crumbs on firmly; refrigerate 1 hour.

Heat oil in pan, add lamb in batches, cook until lightly browned. Transfer to baking sheet in single layer, bake, un-covered in 375°F oven 5 minutes, drain on absorbent paper. Cut lamb evenly into ½ inch slices.

Using a vegetable peeler, cut peel thinly from lemons and limes, avoiding white pith; cut peel into thin strips. Add peel to pan of boiling water, boil 30 seconds; drain, rinse under cold water, drain. Combine arugula, sprouts and peel, top with lamb; drizzle with dressing. Serve with tahini dip.

Dressing: Combine all ingredients in screw-top jar; shake well.

Tahini Dip: Combine all ingredients in bowl; mix well.

Serves 6.

PORK AND VEAL SALAD WITH EGGPLANT CRISPS

3 tablespoons olive oil
1 onion, finely chopped
4 cloves garlic, minced
¼ cup pine nuts
¾lb ground pork and veal
¼ cup shredded fresh basil
⅔ cup grated Parmesan cheese
1½ bunches (about 6oz) arugula
¼ cup Parmesan cheese flakes

EGGPLANT CRISPS
1 large eggplant, thinly sliced
oil for deep-frying

TOMATO VINAIGRETTE
3 tomatoes, chopped
4 teaspoons olive oil
2 teaspoons balsamic vinegar

Heat oil in skillet, add onion, garlic and pine nuts, cook, stirring, until onion is soft. Add pork and veal, cook, stirring, until cooked; cool.

Stir in basil and grated cheese. Serve pork and veal mixture on arugula leaves, top with eggplant crisps and cheese flakes; drizzle with tomato vinaigrette.
Eggplant Crisps: Deep-fry eggplant slices in batches in hot oil until browned and crisp; drain on absorbent paper.
Tomato Vinaigrette: Blend or process all ingredients until well combined. Push tomato mixture through sieve; discard pulp and seeds.
Serves 4.

MEXICAN-STYLE TACOS WITH ANCHOVY DRESSING

6 slices bacon, chopped
¼ small cabbage, shredded
1 cup (about 1½oz) firmly packed
    watercress sprigs
1 teaspoon sambal oelek
3 radishes, grated
1 small red bell pepper,
    finely chopped
1 avocado, chopped
8 jumbo taco shells

ANCHOVY DRESSING
2 anchovy fillets
1 clove garlic, minced
4 teaspoons white wine vinegar
¼ cup olive oil
¼ cup thickened cream
1 teaspoon chopped fresh oregano

Add bacon to dry skillet, stir over heat until crisp; drain on absorbent paper. Combine bacon, cabbage, watercress, sambal oelek, radishes and pepper in bowl, mix well; gently stir in avocado. Crisp taco shells in oven, following directions on package. Fill taco shells with bacon mixture; drizzle with anchovy dressing.
Anchovy Dressing: Blend or process anchovy fillets, garlic, vinegar, oil and cream until smooth; stir in oregano.
Serves 4.

WARM LENTIL AND SAUSAGE SALAD

4 teaspoons olive oil
5 smoky pork sausages
1¼ cups (½lb) brown lentils
14½oz can tomatoes
1 teaspoon sugar
2¼ cups water
2 cloves garlic, minced
1 bay leaf
4 teaspoons olive oil, extra
1 onion, chopped
3 slices bacon, chopped
1 red bell pepper, chopped
1 green bell pepper, chopped

Heat oil in skillet, add sausages, cook until browned and cooked through; drain on absorbent paper. Cut into ½ inch slices.

Combine lentils, undrained crushed tomatoes, sugar, water, garlic and bay leaf in pan, simmer, covered, about 35 minutes or until lentils are just tender and liquid is absorbed.

Heat extra oil in skillet, add onion and bacon, cook, stirring, until onion is soft. Add sausages and peppers, cook, stirring, until sausages are heated through. Combine sausage mixture and lentil mixture in bowl; mix gently. Serve salad warm, or cold if desired.

Serves 4.

LEFT: Clockwise from left: Pork and Veal Salad with Eggplant Crisps, Warm Lentil and Sausage Salad, Mexican-Style Tacos with Anchovy Dressing.

SPICY SAUSAGE AND PEA SALAD

1 cup (6oz) dried black-eyed peas
3 cups chicken broth
4 teaspoons olive oil
11oz hot csabai sausage, sliced
1 onion, thinly sliced
1 red bell pepper, chopped
1 green bell pepper, chopped
1 large zucchini, chopped
½ cup Parmesan cheese flakes
12 black olives, pitted, quartered
⅓ cup shredded fresh basil

DRESSING
2 tomatoes, chopped
¼ cup olive oil
1 clove garlic, minced
2 teaspoons red wine vinegar
½ teaspoon sugar

Place peas in bowl, cover well with water, cover, stand overnight.

Drain peas, combine with broth in pan, simmer, covered, about 25 minutes or until peas are just tender; drain, cool.

Heat oil in pan, add sausage and onion, cook, stirring, until sausage is slightly crisp; drain on absorbent paper, cool. Combine peas, sausage mixture, remaining ingredients and dressing in bowl; mix well.
Dressing: Blend or process tomatoes until smooth, strain. Combine tomato puree with remaining ingredients in screw-top jar; shake well.

Serves 4.

TORTELLINI SALAD WITH TOMATOES AND BASIL

2lb pork and veal tortellini
4 large tomatoes, peeled, seeded, chopped
1 red onion, chopped
1 cup (5oz) black olives, pitted, sliced
¼ cup shredded fresh basil
3 tablespoons chopped fresh chives
2 cloves garlic, minced
½ cup olive oil
3 tablespoons white wine vinegar
¼ teaspoon freshly ground black pepper

Add tortellini to large pan of boiling water, boil, uncovered, until tender; drain, rinse under cold water, drain. Combine tortellini with remaining ingredients in bowl; mix well. Cover, refrigerate until cold.

Serves 4.

BELOW: Spicy Sausage and Pea Salad.
RIGHT: From left: Tortellini Salad with Tomatoes and Basil, Veal with Noodles and Bean Salad.

VEAL WITH NOODLES AND BEAN SALAD

Veal can be marinated a day ahead; store, covered, in refrigerator.

1lb veal tenderloin
½ cup dried adzuki beans
3 tablespoons light olive oil
10oz long beans
1lb thick egg noodles
2 teaspoons cornstarch
½ cup water
1 teaspoon sugar
4 teaspoons light soy sauce

MARINADE
1 orange
½ cup fresh orange juice
4 teaspoons grated fresh gingerroot
3 tablespoons honey
4 teaspoons Dijon mustard

Combine veal and marinade in bowl, cover, refrigerate several hours.

Cover adzuki beans with water in bowl, stand 3 hours. Drain adzuki beans, rinse well. Add adzuki beans to pan of water, bring to boil, simmer, uncovered, about 30 minutes or until tender; drain.

Remove veal from marinade, discard peel, reserve remaining marinade for sauce. Heat oil in roasting pan, add veal, cook until browned all over. Transfer pan to 400°F oven, bake veal, uncovered, about 15 minutes or until veal is cooked as desired; cool.

Cut long beans into 3 inch lengths. Boil, steam or microwave long beans until tender; drain, rinse under cold water, drain. Add noodles to pan of boiling water, boil, uncovered, until tender, drain.

Combine reserved marinade, blended cornstarch and water, sugar and soy sauce in pan, stir over heat until sauce boils and thickens slightly, cool. Combine noodles, adzuki beans and long beans, serve with sliced veal and sauce.

Marinade: Cut peel from orange using a vegetable peeler. Combine peel and remaining ingredients in bowl.

Serves 4.

BABY BEET AND PEPPERONI SALAD

Beans best prepared a day ahead; store, covered, at room temperature.

¾ cup dried red beans
5oz pepperoni salami
12 drained artichoke hearts, halved
10oz button mushrooms, quartered
3 bunches (about 15) baby beets

DRESSING
⅔ cup extra virgin olive oil
3 tablespoons balsamic vinegar
3 tablespoons fresh lemon juice
3 tablespoons seeded mustard
½ teaspoon sugar

Place beans in bowl, cover well with water, cover, stand overnight.

Drain beans, add beans to pan of water, simmer, uncovered, about 35 minutes or until tender, drain well. Cut salami into ¼ inch slices, then cut each piece in half. Combine beans, salami, artichoke hearts, mushrooms and ⅓ cup of the dressing in bowl; mix well. Cover, refrigerate several hours or overnight.

Trim leaves from beets, reserve 16 leaves. Add reserved leaves to pan of boiling water, drain immediately, rinse under cold water, drain. Trim stalks about 1¼ inches from beets. Boil, steam or microwave beets until tender; drain, peel.

Add bean mixture to pan, cook, stirring, until heated through, stir in reserved leaves. Serve bean mixture topped with beets; drizzle with remaining dressing.
Dressing: Combine all ingredients in screw-top jar; shake well.

Serves 4.

PIZZAS WITH SUN-DRIED TOMATOES AND PROSCIUTTO

1 package (¼oz) active dry yeast
½ teaspoon sugar
¾ cup warm water
2 cups all-purpose flour
1 teaspoon salt
3 tablespoons olive oil
⅓ cup hummus

TOPPING
5oz sliced prosciutto
¾ cup drained sun-dried tomatoes, sliced
⅔ cup black olives
3 tablespoons olive oil
4 green onions, sliced
10 spinach leaves, shredded
3 tablespoons shredded fresh basil

Combine yeast, sugar and water in small bowl, cover, stand in warm place about 10 minutes or until frothy.

Sift flour and salt into bowl, stir in yeast mixture and oil, mix to a soft dough. Turn dough onto lightly floured surface, knead about 5 minutes or until smooth.

Place dough in lightly oiled bowl, cover, stand in warm place about 1 hour or until dough is doubled in size.

Knead dough on floured surface until smooth. Divide dough into 4 portions. Roll each portion into a 6½ inch round, place rounds onto oiled baking sheets, prick lightly with fork. Bake in 400°F oven about 10 minutes or until browned and crisp; cool. Spread 4 teaspoons of hummus onto each pizza base, spoon over topping.
Topping: Slice prosciutto into thin strips, add to dry pan, cook, stirring, until crisp; drain. Combine prosciutto and remaining ingredients in bowl; mix well.

Serves 4.

RIGHT: From left: Pizzas with Sun-Dried Tomatoes and Prosciutto, Baby Beet and Pepperoni Salad.

PEPPERED PORK WITH RASPBERRY VINAIGRETTE

1¼lb pork tenderloins
4 teaspoons cracked
   black peppercorns
1 tablespoon dried juniper
   berries, minced
3 tablespoons olive oil
½ bunch (10oz) spinach
1 small red oak leaf lettuce
1 small romaine lettuce
7oz fresh blueberries
7oz fresh raspberries

RASPBERRY VINAIGRETTE
2½oz fresh raspberries
3 tablespoons raspberry vinegar
⅔ cup olive oil
2 teaspoons sugar

Toss pork in combined peppercorns and juniper berries to coat. Heat oil in skillet, add pork, cook until browned all over. Transfer pork to wire rack in roasting pan, bake, uncovered, in 400°F oven about 15 minutes or until pork is just cooked; cool. Serve sliced pork with torn spinach, lettuce leaves and berries; drizzle with raspberry vinaigrette.
Raspberry Vinaigrette: Blend or process berries until smooth, strain; discard seeds. Combine puree with remaining ingredients in screw-top jar; shake well.
Serves 4 to 6.

BARBEQUED PORK AND CHINESE CABBAGE SALAD

4½ inch piece (about ¼lb)
   fresh gingerroot
3 cloves garlic
oil for deep-frying
¼ bunch garlic chives
1¼lb Chinese barbequed pork, sliced
1 Chinese cabbage, sliced
3 cups (about ½lb) bean sprouts
1 cup (about 2½oz) snow pea sprouts
7oz snow peas, halved diagonally
¾ cup roasted peanuts
½ cup whole fresh cilantro leaves
½ cup whole fresh mint leaves

RED ONION PICKLE
½ cup rice vinegar
¼ cup mirin
¼ cup dry red wine
1 clove garlic, sliced
⅛ teaspoon chili flakes
3 tablespoons sugar
¼ teaspoon cracked
   black peppercorns
1 red onion, sliced

DRESSING
⅓ cup light soy sauce
3 tablespoons Oriental sesame oil
4 teaspoons sugar
⅓ cup cider vinegar
⅓ cup light olive oil

Cut gingerroot into thin strips. Cut garlic into thin slices. Deep-fry gingerroot and garlic in hot oil until lightly browned; drain well. Cut garlic chives into ¾ inch lengths.

Combine half the gingerroot and garlic with garlic chives, pork, cabbage, bean sprouts, snow pea sprouts, snow peas, peanuts, herbs and red onion pickle in bowl, add dressing; mix well. Sprinkle with remaining gingerroot and garlic.
Red Onion Pickle: Combine vinegar, mirin, wine, garlic, chili flakes, sugar and peppercorns in pan, simmer, uncovered, 2 minutes. Add onion, cook, covered, until onion is soft; cool. Drain onion, reserve ¼ cup pickling liquid for dressing.
Dressing: Combine reserved pickling liquid and remaining ingredients in screw-top jar; shake well.
Serves 6.

PICNIC LOAF

Recipe best prepared a day ahead; store, covered, in refrigerator.

1 large eggplant, sliced
coarse (kosher) salt
2 red bell peppers
1 green bell pepper
1 yellow bell pepper
3 tablespoons olive oil
2 tablespoons (¼ stick) butter
2 cloves garlic, minced
4 zucchini, sliced
2 baguette loaves
¼ cup sun-dried tomato paste
5oz sliced spicy salami
12 black olives, pitted, sliced
¼ cup drained sun-dried
   tomatoes, chopped

Sprinkle eggplant slices with salt, stand 1 hour. Rinse under cold water, pat dry with absorbent paper. Broil eggplant slices in batches until lightly browned.

Cut peppers in half lengthways, remove seeds and membranes. Broil peppers, skin-side-up, until skin blisters and blackens. Peel away skin, cut peppers into strips. Heat oil, butter and garlic in pan, add zucchini, cook in batches until lightly browned, drain on absorbent paper; cool.

Cut loaves in half horizontally. Broil cut sides of bread until lightly toasted, brush evenly with tomato paste. Cover 2 bread halves with salami, top with eggplant, peppers, zucchini, olives, sun-dried tomatoes and remaining bread halves; wrap firmly in foil. Place loaves on tray, place weight on top to flatten loaves; refrigerate overnight.

Serves 6 to 8.

FAR LEFT: From back: Barbequed Pork and Chinese Cabbage Salad; Peppered Pork with Raspberry Vinaigrette.
LEFT: Picnic Loaf.

CREAMY GNOCCHI AND HAM SALAD

1lb gnocchi
2 tablespoons (¼ stick) butter
2 cloves garlic, minced
1lb button mushrooms, sliced
4 slices bacon, chopped
1lb broccoli, chopped
¼lb snow peas, sliced
½lb cooked ham pieces, chopped

DRESSING
½ cup cream
3 tablespoons sour cream
1 teaspoon Dijon mustard
4 teaspoons seeded mustard
2 teaspoons honey
⅓ cup chopped fresh parsley

Add gnocchi to large pan of boiling water, boil, uncovered, until just tender, drain.

Heat butter in skillet, add garlic and mushrooms, cook, stirring, until mushrooms are soft and liquid is evaporated; remove from skillet. Add bacon to same skillet, cook, stirring, until browned and crisp; drain on absorbent paper. Boil, steam or microwave broccoli until just tender; drain, rinse under cold water, drain well.

Combine gnocchi, mushroom mixture, bacon, broccoli, snow peas and ham in bowl, add dressing; mix gently.
Dressing: Combine all ingredients in bowl; mix well.

Serves 4.

PORK WITH RED CABBAGE AND RAISIN SALAD

Raisins best prepared a day ahead; store, covered, at room temperature.

½ cup dark seedless raisins
¼ cup port wine
½ red apple
1 green apple
1¼lb roasted pork, chopped
½ red cabbage, finely shredded
1½ cups (5oz) pecans or walnuts
4 green onions, sliced
4 teaspoons caraway seeds

DRESSING
1 egg yolk
3 tablespoons cider vinegar
3 tablespoons sweet alcoholic cider
1 teaspoon French mustard
3 tablespoons apple juice
1 cup olive oil

Combine raisins and port wine in bowl, cover, stand several hours or overnight.

Drain raisins, discard port wine. Core apples, cut into thin wedges. Combine raisins, apples and remaining ingredients in bowl, add dressing; mix well.
Dressing: Blend egg yolk, vinegar, cider, mustard and juice until smooth, gradually add oil in thin stream while motor is operating, blend until slightly thickened.

Serves 6.

HAM AND PICKLED PEAR SALAD

1lb sliced cooked leg ham
2 cups firmly packed watercress sprigs
8 radishes, quartered
4 teaspoons pecans or walnuts, chopped

PICKLED PEARS
2 pears
3 tablespoons finely chopped fresh gingerroot
1 cup water
2 cups cider vinegar
1½ cups sugar
1 cinnamon stick
3 star anise
1 teaspoon cloves

DRESSING
⅓ cup light olive oil
3 tablespoons chopped fresh chives

Cut ham into thin strips. Combine ham, watercress, radishes, nuts and half the dressing in bowl; mix gently. Top with sliced pickled pears; drizzle with remaining dressing.
Pickled Pears: Peel pears, halve and remove cores. Combine gingerroot, water, vinegar, sugar, cinnamon, star anise and cloves in pan. Stir over heat, without boiling, until sugar is dissolved, add pears, simmer, covered, about 5 minutes or until pears are tender; cool in poaching liquid. Drain pears, reserve ⅔ cup liquid for dressing.
Dressing: Combine reserved poaching liquid, oil and chives in screw-top jar; shake well.

Serves 4.

RIGHT: Clockwise from left: Ham and Pickled Pear Salad, Pork with Red Cabbage and Raisin Salad, Creamy Gnocchi and Ham Salad.

SMOKED CHICKEN AND HAM WITH FIGS

2 avocados
4 teaspoons fresh lemon juice
1 bunch chicory
1 cup (about 1½oz) firmly packed
    watercress sprigs
4 smoked boneless, skinless chicken
    breast halves, sliced
12 slices double-smoked ham
4 fresh figs, halved
½ cup roasted hazelnuts, halved

DRESSING
¼ cup olive oil
4 teaspoons fresh lemon juice
⅛ teaspoon sugar

Chop avocados into 1½ inch pieces, brush with juice.

Place avocado, chicory, watercress, chicken, ham and figs on plate, sprinkle with nuts; drizzle with dressing.
Dressing: Combine all ingredients in screw-top jar; shake well.

Serves 4.

LEFT: From back: Warm Chicken and Nectarine Salad, Smoked Chicken and Ham with Figs.
BELOW: Tropical Chicken Salad.

WARM CHICKEN AND NECTARINE SALAD

2 oranges
2 tomatoes
2 nectarines
2 tablespoons (¼ stick) butter
4 boneless, skinless chicken breast
    halves
3 tablespoons red wine vinegar
1 small red leaf lettuce
1 small Boston lettuce

ORANGE YOGURT DRESSING
3 tablespoons plain yogurt
¼ cup fresh orange juice
3 tablespoons sour cream
2 teaspoons chopped fresh mint
4 teaspoons chopped fresh chives

Using a vegetable peeler, cut peel thinly from oranges, avoiding white pith; cut peel into thin strips. Cut tomatoes and nectarines into thin wedges.

Heat butter in skillet, add chicken, cook until browned and cooked through. Remove chicken from skillet, slice lengthways. Add vinegar and peel to skillet, simmer, uncovered, for 30 seconds.

Top torn lettuce leaves with tomatoes, nectarines and chicken; drizzle with peel mixture. Serve warm chicken and nectarine salad with orange yogurt dressing.
Orange Yogurt Dressing: Combine all ingredients in bowl, mix well; cover, refrigerate 30 minutes.

Serves 4.

TROPICAL CHICKEN SALAD

1 large lime
2 boneless, skinless chicken breasts
2 cups chicken broth
1lb sweet potato
7oz snow peas

DRESSING
3 tablespoons salad oil
1 onion, finely chopped
1 clove garlic, minced
⅓ cup fresh lime juice
1⅔ cups canned unsweetened
    coconut cream
¼ cup shredded coconut
2 teaspoons sugar

Cut peel thinly from lime, avoiding white pith; cut peel into thin strips. Place chicken in pan in single layer, pour over enough broth to just cover chicken, simmer, about 10 minutes or until cooked; cool in broth.

Cut potato evenly into ¾ inch pieces. Boil, steam or microwave potato and snow peas separately until tender; drain, rinse under cold water, drain. Cut snow peas diagonally. Cut chicken into ¾ inch pieces. Combine peel, potato, snow peas and chicken in bowl, add dressing; mix gently.
Dressing: Heat oil in pan, add onion and garlic, cook, stirring, until onion is soft. Add remaining ingredients, simmer, uncovered, about 5 minutes or until mixture is thickened slightly; cool.

Serves 4 to 6.

ORIENTAL CHICKEN AND SHRIMP SALAD

Chicken can be marinated a day ahead; store, covered, in refrigerator.

1¼lb chicken thighs, boned, skinned, thinly sliced
¼ cup light soy sauce
4 teaspoons oyster-flavored sauce
½ teaspoon five-spice powder
4 teaspoons dry sherry
2 cloves garlic, minced
1 teaspoon grated fresh gingerroot
cornstarch
oil for deep-frying
1lb fresh egg noodles
1lb cooked shrimp
3½oz snow peas
2 cups (about 5oz) bean sprouts
8oz can bamboo shoots, rinsed, drained
2½oz snow pea sprouts
1 small red bell pepper, thinly sliced
⅔ cup slivered almonds, toasted

DRESSING
3 tablespoons light soy sauce
½ teaspoon Oriental sesame oil
⅓ cup salad oil
1 teaspoon fish sauce
1 teaspoon honey
1 clove garlic, minced
4 teaspoons fresh lemon juice

Combine chicken, sauces, spice powder, sherry, garlic and gingerroot in bowl; cover, refrigerate several hours or overnight.

Drain chicken, discard marinade. Toss chicken in cornstarch, shake away excess cornstarch. Deep-fry chicken in batches in hot oil until well browned and cooked through; drain on absorbent paper.

Add noodles to pan of boiling water, boil, uncovered, until tender; drain, rinse under cold water, drain well. Shell shrimp, leaving tails intact. Add peas to pan of boiling water, cook 30 seconds; drain, rinse under cold water, drain well.

Combine chicken, noodles, shrimp, peas, bean sprouts, bamboo shoots, snow pea sprouts, pepper and nuts in bowl, add dressing; mix well.

Dressing: Combine all ingredients in screw-top jar; shake well.

Serves 4.

CHICKEN AND BELL PEPPERS WITH HAZELNUT DRESSING

2 yellow bell peppers
2 red bell peppers
2 green bell peppers
2 cloves garlic, minced
4 teaspoons seeded mustard
4 boneless, skinless chicken breast halves
4 teaspoons hazelnut oil
3 tablespoons butter
3 bunches (about ½lb) sorrel

HAZELNUT DRESSING
⅓ cup (1½oz) hazelnuts
¼ cup hazelnut oil
¼ cup salad oil
3 tablespoons white wine vinegar
¼ cup golden raisins
1 clove garlic, peeled, quartered
4 teaspoons fresh thyme sprigs
¼ teaspoon sugar

Quarter peppers, remove seeds and membranes. Broil peppers, skin-side-up, until skin blisters and blackens. Peel away skin, cut peppers into strips.

Spread combined garlic and mustard over both sides of chicken. Heat oil and butter in skillet, add chicken, cook on both sides until browned and cooked through, drain on absorbent paper; cool. Cut chicken into long thin slices. Top sorrel leaves with chicken and peppers, drizzle with hazelnut dressing.

Hazelnut Dressing: Spread hazelnuts onto baking sheet, bake in 375°F oven 5 minutes. Place hazelnuts on kitchen towel, rub firmly to remove skins. Return hazelnuts to baking sheet, bake further 3 minutes or until lightly browned.

Combine oils, vinegar, raisins, garlic, thyme and sugar in screw-top jar, stand several hours. Just before serving, discard garlic, add hazelnuts; shake well.

Serves 4.

QUAIL WITH PROSCIUTTO AND PESTO DRESSING

8 quail
8 slices prosciutto
2 bunches (about ½lb) arugula
½ cup Parmesan cheese flakes
⅓ cup (1½oz) pine nuts, toasted

PESTO DRESSING
1 cup firmly packed fresh basil leaves
2 cloves garlic, minced
3 tablespoons pine nuts
¼ cup grated Parmesan cheese
¾ cup olive oil

Using sharp knife or scissors, cut down each side of backbone of quail; flatten quail, discard backbones. Broil or barbeque quail until browned and cooked. Broil prosciutto until lightly browned. Place quail and prosciutto on arugula, sprinkle with cheese flakes and nuts; drizzle with pesto dressing.

Pesto Dressing: Blend or process basil, garlic, nuts and cheese with ¼ cup of the oil until smooth. Gradually add remaining oil in a stream while motor is operating; blend until smooth.

Serves 4.

LEFT: Oriental Chicken and Shrimp Salad.
RIGHT: From back: Quail with Prosciutto and Pesto Dressing, Chicken and Bell Peppers with Hazelnut Dressing.

CHICKEN TONNATO

**4 boneless, skinless chicken
    breast halves**
2 cups chicken broth, approximately
2 red bell peppers
2 green bell peppers
1 red oak leaf lettuce
2 Boston lettuce
4 teaspoons drained capers

TUNA MAYONNAISE
1 egg yolk
¼ cup olive oil
¼ cup salad oil
1 clove garlic, minced
2 teaspoons fresh lemon juice
**4 teaspoons drained
    capers, chopped**
6½oz can tuna, drained

Place chicken in pan in single layer, add enough broth to barely cover chicken. Simmer, uncovered, about 10 minutes, turning once, or until chicken is cooked through; cool chicken in broth.

Cut peppers in half, remove seeds and membranes, broil peppers, skin-side-up, until skin blisters and blackens. Peel away skin, cut peppers into ¾ inch strips. Cut chicken lengthways into thin slices. Serve chicken on lettuce leaves with peppers and capers; top with tuna mayonnaise.
Tuna Mayonnaise: Blend or process egg yolk until smooth. Add combined oils gradually in a thin stream while motor is operating; add garlic, juice, capers and tuna, blend until smooth.

Serves 4.

MARINATED CHICKEN AND GOATS' CHEESE SALAD

**5 boneless, skinless chicken breast
    halves, sliced**
3 tablespoons light soy sauce
3 tablespoons olive oil
3 tablespoons fresh lemon juice
4 teaspoons seasoned pepper
4 teaspoons olive oil, extra
1lb green beans
**1 cup (5oz) unsalted
    roasted cashews**
3½oz goats' cheese, crumbled

DRESSING
4 teaspoons Dijon mustard
3 tablespoons balsamic vinegar
⅓ cup olive oil
2 green onions, chopped
4 teaspoons fresh lemon juice

Combine chicken, sauce, oil, juice and pepper in bowl, cover, refrigerate 1 hour.

Heat extra oil in skillet, add undrained chicken in batches, cook until tender; cool. Cut beans into 1¼ inch pieces. Boil, steam or microwave beans until just tender; drain, rinse under cold water, drain.

Combine chicken, beans and nuts in bowl, add dressing, mix well; serve sprinkled with cheese.
Dressing: Combine all ingredients in screw-top jar; shake well.

Serves 4.

CURRIED CHICKEN AND PASTA SALAD

2 cups (5oz) shell pasta
4 teaspoons light olive oil
3 tablespoons curry powder
4 green onions, chopped
1 small red bell pepper, chopped
1 small green bell pepper, chopped
½ cup mayonnaise
½ cup light sour cream
**2 cups (14oz) chopped cooked
    chicken**
8 Boston lettuce leaves

Add pasta to large pan of boiling water, boil, uncovered, until tender; drain, rinse under cold water, drain.

Heat oil in skillet, add curry powder, onions and peppers, cook, stirring, 1 minute; cool. Combine pasta, curry mixture, mayonnaise, sour cream and chicken in bowl; mix well. Serve curried chicken mixture on lettuce leaves.

Serves 4.

LEFT: Clockwise from top: Curried Chicken and Pasta Salad, Marinated Chicken and Goats' Cheese Salad, Chicken Tonnato.

WARM CHICKEN LIVER AND PISTACHIO SALAD

2 tablespoons (¼ stick) butter
1lb chicken livers
4 teaspoons chopped fresh thyme
¼ cup red wine vinegar
4 teaspoons olive oil
⅓ cup (1½oz) pistachios, toasted
1 tablespoon butter, extra
1½ bunches (about ¾lb) mizuna
7oz fresh raspberries

Heat butter in skillet, add livers and thyme, cook, stirring, about 4 minutes or until livers are browned and cooked; remove livers from skillet. Add vinegar, oil and pistachios to skillet, cook, stirring, until mixture boils, reduce heat, quickly stir in extra butter. Top mizuna with livers, drizzle with pistachio mixture, serve with raspberries.
Serves 4.

TURKEY, BELL PEPPER AND TARRAGON SALAD

3 slices bacon, chopped
2 large red bell peppers
3 stalks celery
14oz sliced roasted turkey
¾ cup brazil nuts, toasted, chopped
4 drained artichoke hearts, sliced
3 cups (about 5oz) firmly packed
**   watercress sprigs**

TARRAGON DRESSING
3 tablespoons chopped
**   fresh tarragon**
2 teaspoons honey
3 tablespoons white wine vinegar
⅓ cup olive oil

Add bacon to dry skillet, cook, stirring, until bacon is crisp; drain on absorbent paper.

Quarter peppers, remove seeds and membranes. Broil peppers, skin-side-up, until skin blisters and blackens. Peel away skin, slice peppers thinly. Cut celery into 2½ inch thin strips. Cut turkey evenly into thin strips.

Combine bacon, peppers, celery, turkey, nuts, artichokes and watercress in bowl; drizzle with tarragon dressing.
Tarragon Dressing: Combine all ingredients in screw-top jar; shake well.
Serves 4.

BELOW: From left: Turkey, Bell Pepper and Tarragon Salad, Warm Chicken Liver and Pistachio Salad.
RIGHT: From left: Smoked Turkey and Belgian Endive Salad, Chicken and Crispy Noodles with Peanut Sauce.

CHICKEN AND CRISPY NOODLES WITH PEANUT SAUCE

1oz rice vermicelli noodles
oil for deep-frying
15oz can baby corn, drained
2½ cups (about 1lb) sliced
    cooked chicken
¾ cup cooked green peas
1⅓ cups (3½oz) shredded
    red cabbage
1⅓ cups (3½oz) shredded
    savoy cabbage
1 cup (2½oz) bean sprouts
4 green onions, chopped
5oz oyster mushrooms, sliced
5 fresh dates, pitted, chopped

PEANUT SAUCE
⅓ cup smooth peanut butter
⅓ cup canned unsweetened
    coconut cream
2 teaspoons light soy sauce
1½ teaspoons sugar
1½ teaspoons fresh lime juice
⅓ cup water, approximately

Break noodles in half, deep-fry in hot oil until puffed and crisp; drain.

Lightly crush noodles. Cut corn in half lengthways. Combine noodles and corn with remaining ingredients in bowl; drizzle with peanut sauce.

Peanut Sauce: Combine peanut butter, coconut cream, sauce, sugar and lime juice in bowl, stir in enough water to give a thin pouring sauce.

Serves 4.

SMOKED TURKEY AND BELGIAN ENDIVE SALAD

1lb sliced smoked turkey breast
3 tablespoons butter
3 tablespoons hazelnut oil
1 clove garlic, minced
1 red apple
6 Belgian endives
⅓ cup roasted hazelnuts, chopped
3 tablespoons chopped fresh chives

DRESSING
¼ cup hazelnut oil
3 tablespoons salad oil
¼ cup raspberry vinegar
½ teaspoon sugar
¼ teaspoon seasoned pepper

Cut turkey into thin strips. Heat butter and oil in skillet, add turkey and garlic, cook, stirring, until turkey is lightly browned; drain well. Cut apple into thin strips.

Combine turkey, apple, endive leaves and nuts in bowl; drizzle with dressing, sprinkle with chives.

Dressing: Combine all ingredients in screw-top jar; shake well.

Serves 4.

HERRING, POTATO AND EGG SALAD

4 (about 7oz) rollmop herrings
10 baby new potatoes
2 apples, halved, sliced
12 drained cocktail onions
5 canned drained baby
beets, quartered
6 hard-boiled eggs, halved

DRESSING
½ cup mayonnaise
¼ cup sour cream
3 tablespoons white wine vinegar
4 teaspoons chopped fresh dill

Unroll herrings, remove dill pickles. Reserve dill pickles for dressing. Cut herrings into strips. Boil, steam or microwave potatoes until tender; drain, cool.

Combine potatoes, apples and half the dressing in bowl; mix gently. Top potato mixture with herrings, onions, beets and eggs; drizzle with remaining dressing.

Dressing: Combine reserved chopped dill pickles and remaining ingredients in bowl; mix well.

Serves 4 to 6.

RIGHT: from left: Herring, Potato and Egg Salad, Poached Fish and Mango with Tandoori Dressing.

POACHED FISH AND MANGO WITH TANDOORI DRESSING

Fish can be marinated a day ahead; store, covered, in refrigerator.

1 teaspoon fish sauce
1 teaspoon light soy sauce
4 teaspoons white wine vinegar
1 teaspoon sugar
4 (about 1¾lb) firm white fish fillets
⅔ cup water
½ large mango, sliced
6 radicchio lettuce leaves
1 small romaine lettuce, shredded
5oz snow pea sprouts
1 small yellow bell pepper, sliced

TANDOORI DRESSING
½ large mango, chopped
⅓ cup plain yogurt
½ teaspoon sugar
½ teaspoon grated fresh gingerroot
1 teaspoon fresh lemon juice
4 teaspoons salad oil
¼ teaspoon turmeric
¼ teaspoon paprika
¼ teaspoon garam masala
¼ teaspoon ground cardamom
⅛ teaspoon chili powder
small pinch ground saffron

Combine sauces, vinegar and sugar in bowl, add fish, cover, refrigerate several hours or overnight.

Drain fish, reserve marinade. Combine reserved marinade and water in pan, bring to boil, add fish, simmer, covered, until fish is just cooked. Drain fish on wire rack, discard poaching liquid. Break fish into pieces. Combine fish, mango, lettuce, sprouts and pepper on plate, top with tandoori dressing.

Tandoori Dressing: Blend or process mango flesh, yogurt, sugar, gingerroot and juice until smooth. Heat oil in skillet, add spices, cook, stirring, until fragrant. Combine mango mixture and spice mixture in bowl, mix well; cover, refrigerate 1 hour.

Serves 4.

CHILI CRAB AND GRAPEFRUIT SALAD

6 large (about 5lb) cooked
    crabs
1 cup (1½oz) firmly packed
    watercress sprigs
1 bunch chicory
2 grapefruit, segmented
¾ cup roasted
    unsalted cashews
3 tablespoons shredded
    coconut, toasted

DRESSING
1 teaspoon fish sauce
1 teaspoon sambal oelek
4 teaspoons fresh lime juice
½ cup canned unsweetened
    coconut milk
4 teaspoons chopped
    fresh cilantro

Remove flesh from crab bodies and legs.
Combine watercress, chicory, grapefruit
and nuts in bowl, top with crab flesh; drizzle with dressing, sprinkle with coconut.
Dressing: Combine all ingredients in
screw-top jar; shake well.

Serves 4.

MARINATED BABY OCTOPUS WITH RED CABBAGE

*Octopus can be marinated a day
ahead; store, covered, in refrigerator.*

2lb baby octopus
2 cloves garlic, minced
⅓ cup hoisin sauce
3 tablespoons dry sherry
1 teaspoon grated fresh gingerroot
3 tablespoons light olive oil
1 red bell pepper, thinly sliced
1 green bell pepper, thinly sliced
½ small red cabbage, shredded

DRESSING
¼ cup rice wine vinegar
2 tablespoons black bean sauce
⅓ cup salad oil
½ teaspoon sambal oelek

Remove and discard heads and beaks
from octopus. Cut octopus in half. Combine octopus, garlic, sauce, sherry and
gingerroot in bowl; cover, refrigerate
several hours or overnight.

Heat oil in skillet, add undrained
octopus in batches, cook until browned
and tender. Serve warm octopus with
combined bell peppers and cabbage;
drizzle with dressing.
Dressing: Combine all ingredients in
screw-top jar; shake well.

Serves 4.

TUNA AND BRAISED ONION SALAD

¼ cup light olive oil
2 tablespoons (¼ stick) butter
3 large onions, sliced
3 tablespoons red wine vinegar
4 (about 1¼lb) tuna steaks
1 bunch (about ¼lb) arugula
½ bunch (about 10oz) spinach,
    shredded

Heat oil and butter in heavy-based skillet,
add onions, cook, covered, stirring occasionally, about 30 minutes or until onions
are very soft. Add vinegar, simmer, uncovered, 1 minute. Add tuna to same skillet, cook, uncovered, until tuna is cooked
as desired. Remove tuna from skillet, cut
into pieces. Serve warm tuna with braised
onions, arugula and spinach.

Serves 4.

*LEFT: From top: Chili Crab and Grapefruit
Salad, Marinated Baby Octopus with
Red Cabbage.
RIGHT: Tuna and Braised Onion Salad.*

FRESH SNAPPER AND SNOW PEA SALAD

**2 firm tomatoes,
    peeled, seeded**
4 zucchini
1 small red bell pepper
**¼ cup finely chopped
    pitted black olives**
2 green onions, chopped
¼ cup (½ stick) butter
4 teaspoons olive oil
1lb snapper fillets
3½oz snow peas, thinly sliced
1 Boston lettuce

DRESSING
¼ cup champagne vinegar
⅔ cup virgin olive oil
2 teaspoons seeded mustard
1 teaspoon honey
1 clove garlic, minced

Finely chop tomatoes, zucchini and pepper; combine in bowl. Stir in olives, onions and ¼ cup of the dressing.

Heat butter and oil in skillet, add fish, cook until just cooked, cool. Slice fish into ¾ inch strips. Add snow peas, fish and torn lettuce leaves to tomato mixture, mix gently; drizzle with remaining dressing.
Dressing: Combine all ingredients in screw-top jar; shake well.

Serves 4.

FRESH SALMON AND PASTA SALAD

6oz pasta shells
1 carrot, finely chopped
2 stalks celery, finely chopped
⅓ cup mayonnaise
3 tablespoons sour cream
½ teaspoon grated lemon zest
¼ teaspoon fish sauce
4 teaspoons fresh lemon juice
1lb salmon fillets

DRESSING
¼ cup fresh lemon juice
¼ cup olive oil
1 teaspoon chopped fresh dill

Add pasta to pan of boiling water, boil, uncovered, until just tender; drain. Combine pasta, carrot, celery, mayonnaise, sour cream, zest, sauce and juice in bowl; cover, refrigerate 1 hour.

Cook salmon in greased, heavy-based skillet or on well-greased barbeque plate until just cooked. Remove skin from salmon; break salmon into pieces. Top pasta salad with salmon; drizzle with dressing.
Dressing: Combine all ingredients in screw-top jar; shake well.

Serves 4.

LEFT: From left: Fresh Salmon and Pasta Salad, Fresh Snapper and Snow Pea Salad.

OPEN HERB RAVIOLI WITH SHRIMP AND PESTO

We used dill, flat-leafed parsley, purple basil, unsprayed marigold, nasturtium and rose petals in this recipe.

²/₃ cup all-purpose flour
1 egg
1 teaspoon olive oil
¼ cup fresh herb leaves and
    flower petals
2½lb cooked medium shrimp
1 green oak leaf lettuce
1 bunch (about ½lb) mizuna
½ cup loosely-packed fresh
    purple basil leaves
2 small avocados, sliced
1 papaya, sliced

PESTO MAYONNAISE
1 cup firmly packed fresh basil leaves
3 tablespoons pine nuts, toasted
2 cloves garlic, minced
¼ cup grated Parmesan cheese
¼ cup olive oil
2 egg yolks
1 teaspoon French mustard
2 teaspoons white wine vinegar
1 cup grapeseed oil

Process flour, egg and oil until combined. Knead dough on lightly floured surface until smooth; cover, refrigerate 30 minutes.

Roll dough through thickest setting on pasta machine until smooth and elastic. Cut into 4 equal portions. Roll each portion through pasta machine until as thin as possible. Sprinkle herbs and flowers over 2 pieces of pasta. Lightly brush the 2 remaining pasta pieces with water, place over herbs, press to seal. Roll pasta once through thinnest setting of machine, cut into twelve 4 inch x 4½ inch rectangles; lightly dust with flour.

Add pasta to large pan of boiling water, simmer, uncovered, about 2 minutes or until just tender; drain, rinse under cold water, drain well. Brush each side of pasta with oil, place each sheet between layers of baking paper until needed.

Shell and devein shrimp, leaving tails intact. Place 1 sheet of pasta on plate, top with some of the lettuce, mizuna, basil, shrimp, avocado and papaya; drizzle with pesto mayonnaise, top with another pasta sheet. Repeat with remaining ingredients on individual plates.

Pesto Mayonnaise: Process basil, nuts, garlic, cheese and olive oil until smooth; reserve pesto. Process yolks, mustard and vinegar until smooth, gradually add grapeseed oil in a thin stream while motor is operating. Combine reserved pesto and mayonnaise in bowl; mix well.

Serves 6.

LEFT: Open Herb Ravioli with Shrimp and Pesto.
RIGHT: Lobster Salad with Red Bell Pepper Mousses.

LOBSTER SALAD WITH RED BELL PEPPER MOUSSES

4 medium (about 1¾lb) uncooked
    lobster tails
3 tablespoons butter
2 cloves garlic, minced
1 large radicchio lettuce
1 bunch (½lb) arugula
⅓ cup drained sun-dried
    tomatoes, sliced
⅓ cup shredded fresh basil leaves

RED BELL PEPPER MOUSSES
4 (about 1¾lb) red bell peppers
¼ cup red wine vinegar
2 teaspoons chicken instant bouillon
1 teaspoon sugar
1 tablespoon unflavored gelatin
2 tablespoons water
1 cup whipping cream

DRESSING
⅓ cup olive oil
4 teaspoons white wine vinegar
¼ teaspoon French mustard

Remove lobster meat from tails in 1 piece. Heat butter and garlic in skillet, add lobster, cook until lightly browned all over. Place lobster on baking sheet, brush with pan juices; bake, uncovered, in 375°F oven about 8 minutes or until lobster is just cooked; cool. Slice lobster thickly. Turn mousses onto plates, surround with torn lettuce leaves, arugula, tomatoes, basil and lobster; drizzle with dressing.

Red Bell Pepper Mousses: Lightly oil 4 molds (½ cup capacity). Quarter peppers, remove seeds and membranes. Broil peppers, skin-side-up, until skin blisters and blackens. Peel skin, chop peppers. Combine peppers, vinegar and instant bouillon in pan, simmer, uncovered, until peppers are soft and liquid is evaporated. Blend or process peppers and sugar until smooth, push through sieve.

Sprinkle gelatin over water in cup, place in pan of simmering water, stir until dissolved; cool slightly. Combine pepper mixture and gelatin in bowl, refrigerate until partly set. Beat cream until soft peaks form, fold into pepper mixture in 2 batches. Divide mixture between prepared molds, cover, refrigerate several hours or until set.

Dressing: Combine all ingredients in screw-top jar; shake well.

Serves 4.

SMOKED TROUT AND CHICORY SALAD

3 small smoked trout
1 bunch chicory
1 radicchio lettuce
1 small green oak leaf lettuce
1 cup (about 1½oz) firmly packed
    watercress sprigs
½lb cherry tomatoes

DRESSING
¼ cup olive oil
3 tablespoons cider vinegar
4 teaspoons fresh lemon juice
4 teaspoons chopped fresh dill

Remove skin and bones from trout; flake flesh. Combine torn chicory and lettuce leaves, watercress and tomatoes in bowl, top with trout; drizzle with dressing.
Dressing: Combine all ingredients in screw-top jar; shake well.
Serves 4.

ORIENTAL SHRIMP, MUSHROOM AND CUCUMBER SALAD

2 x ½lb packages Japanese
    dried noodles
4 teaspoons Oriental sesame oil
2lb cooked medium shrimp
1½oz Chinese dried mushrooms
½ cup light soy sauce
1 cup water
4 teaspoons grated fresh gingerroot
2 cloves garlic, minced
3 tablespoons dark brown sugar
½ teaspoon five-spice powder
6 green onions, chopped
1 cup (about 2½oz) bean sprouts
1 long thin green cucumber,
    thinly sliced

Add noodles to large pan of boiling water, boil, uncovered, until tender; drain, rinse under cold water, drain. Combine noodles and oil in bowl.

Shell and devein shrimp, leaving tails intact. Place mushrooms in heatproof bowl, cover with boiling water, stand 20 minutes; drain mushrooms, discard liquid, trim away stems. Combine mushrooms, sauce, water, gingerroot, garlic, sugar and spice powder in pan, simmer, uncovered, about 5 minutes or until reduced by one-third. Combine noodle mixture, mushroom mixture, shrimp, onions and bean sprouts in bowl; mix well. Serve warm noodle mixture with cucumber.
Serves 4.

BELOW: From left: Oriental Shrimp, Mushroom and Cucumber Salad, Smoked Trout and Chicory Salad.
RIGHT: Nutty Sardines with Snow Pea Salad.

NUTTY SARDINES WITH SNOW PEA SALAD

16 (about 1lb) fresh sardines
all-purpose flour
2 eggs, lightly beaten
1½ cups (3½oz) fresh bread crumbs
½ cup finely chopped macadamias
2 teaspoons grated lemon zest
4 teaspoons chopped fresh thyme
oil for deep-frying

SNOW PEA SALAD
1 small leek
5oz snow peas
⅔ cup (3½oz) macadamias, toasted, halved
½ cup sour cream
1 teaspoon grated lemon zest
2 tablespoons fresh lemon juice
2 teaspoons chopped fresh thyme
½ teaspoon honey

LEMON DRESSING
2 tablespoons fresh lemon juice
3 tablespoons salad oil
1 teaspoon honey

Remove sardine heads and entrails.

Cut through underside to backbone; rinse under cold water. Cut backbone

through at tail end without piercing skin. Pull backbone out towards head end to remove. Remove small bones. Pat dry with absorbent paper.

Toss sardines in flour, shake away excess flour. Dip sardines into egg then combined bread crumbs, nuts, zest and thyme. Deep-fry sardines in hot oil until lightly browned; drain on absorbent paper. Serve sardines with snow pea salad and lemon dressing.

Snow Pea Salad: Cut leek and snow peas into thin strips. Combine leek, snow peas and remaining ingredients in bowl; mix well.

Lemon Dressing: Combine all ingredients in screw-top jar; shake well.

Serves 4.

SEAFOOD, POTATO AND WATER CHESTNUT SALAD

1lb baby new potatoes, halved
3½oz sugar snap peas
2oz green beans, halved
2 limes
1¾lb uncooked medium shrimp
⅓ cup olive oil
6 cloves garlic, minced
2 teaspoons cuminseed
14oz sea scallops
½ cup fresh lime juice
4 teaspoons honey
4 teaspoons chopped fresh mint
4 teaspoons chopped
   fresh cilantro
8oz can whole water
   chestnuts, sliced
1 green oak leaf lettuce

Boil, steam or microwave potatoes, peas and beans separately until just tender; drain, rinse under cold water, drain, cool.

Using vegetable peeler, cut peel thinly from limes, avoiding any white pith; cut peel into thin strips. Shell and devein shrimp, leaving tails intact.

Heat oil in skillet, add garlic and seeds, cook, stirring, until fragrant. Add shrimp and scallops, cook, stirring, 2 minutes. Add peel, juice, honey and herbs, cook, stirring, until shrimp and scallops are just cooked; cool. Combine potatoes, peas, beans, shrimp mixture and water chestnuts in bowl, serve on lettuce leaves.

Serves 4.

SOY AND LEMON SEAFOOD WITH SESAME VEGETABLES

10oz cleaned squid
1lb uncooked medium shrimp
1lb sea scallops
3 tablespoons light soy sauce
3 tablespoons fresh lemon juice
4 teaspoons chopped fresh
   lemon grass
3 tablespoons olive oil
4 teaspoons olive oil, extra

SESAME VEGETABLES
2 carrots
1 large red bell pepper
2 zucchini
2 stalks celery
6 spears fresh asparagus
1 tablespoon butter
3 tablespoons sesame seeds, toasted

DRESSING
⅓ cup olive oil
4 teaspoons fresh lemon juice
4 teaspoons light soy sauce
¼ teaspoon Oriental sesame oil
⅛ teaspoon five-spice powder
½ teaspoon sugar

Cut squid into 1¼ inch pieces, score shallow diagonal slashes in diamond pattern on inside surface of squid. Shell and devein shrimp. Combine squid, shrimp, scallops, sauce, juice, lemon grass and oil in bowl; mix well. Cover, refrigerate 1 hour. Drain, discard marinade.

Heat extra oil in skillet, add seafood, cook, stirring, few minutes or until seafood is just cooked. Serve warm seafood with sesame vegetables; top with dressing.

Sesame Vegetables: Cut carrots, pepper, zucchini, celery and asparagus into thin strips. Heat butter in wok, add vegetables and seeds, stir-fry until vegetables are just tender.

Dressing: Combine all ingredients in screw-top jar; shake well.

Serves 4.

WARM SEAFOOD SALAD WITH CURRY BUTTER

We used unsprayed edible flower petals in this recipe; for example, borage, nasturtiums, lavender and rose petals.

1¼lb cooked lobster tails
10oz medium uncooked shrimp
4 teaspoons light olive oil
7oz sea scallops
3½oz lambs' lettuce
1 small lollo rosso lettuce
1 small romaine lettuce
½ cup fresh flower petals

CURRY BUTTER
7oz butter
4 teaspoons curry powder
1 tablespoon honey
½ teaspoon French mustard
4 teaspoons chopped
   fresh cilantro

DRESSING
2 tablespoons red wine vinegar
½ teaspoon French mustard
⅓ cup olive oil

Remove flesh from lobster tail shells, discard shells, cut flesh into chunks. Shell and devein shrimp, leaving tails intact.

Heat oil in skillet, add shrimp and scallops in batches, cook, stirring gently, until just cooked. Add lobster flesh to skillet, cook gently until heated through. Transfer seafood to shallow heatproof dish, top with curry butter, broil until butter just starts to melt. Combine torn lettuce leaves and dressing on plate, sprinkle with flower petals, top with seafood in curry butter.

Curry Butter: Beat butter in small bowl with electric mixer until light and fluffy, add curry powder, honey, mustard and cilantro, beat until combined.

Dressing: Combine all ingredients in screw-top jar; shake well.

Serves 4.

CHILI LIME SEAFOOD WITH SEED CRACKERS

Seafood best prepared a day ahead; store, covered, in refrigerator.

4 (about 14oz) white fish fillets
1lb uncooked medium shrimp
2 eggs
3 tablespoons all-purpose flour
1 teaspoon celery salt
oil for shallow-frying

MARINADE
½ cup light olive oil
2 teaspoons cuminseed, crushed
2 teaspoons coriander seeds
2 cloves garlic, sliced
2 small red chili peppers, finely chopped
1 teaspoon grated lime zest
⅓ cup fresh lime juice
⅓ cup fresh orange juice
½ cup red wine vinegar
2 teaspoons sugar
1 teaspoon paprika

SAUTEED LEEKS
2 leeks
2 tablespoons (¼ stick) butter

SEED CRACKERS
1 cup all-purpose flour
2 tablespoons (¼ stick) butter
1 egg, lightly beaten
4 teaspoons water
2 teaspoons milk
4 teaspoons coarse sea salt
4 teaspoons poppy seeds
4 teaspoons sesame seeds

Remove and discard skin and bones from fillets. Cut each fillet diagonally into ½ inch strips. Shell and devein shrimp, leaving tails intact. Combine eggs, flour and salt in bowl, beat until smooth. Add fish and shrimp, mix lightly to coat.

Shallow-fry fish and shrimp in batches in hot oil until lightly browned; drain on absorbent paper. Combine fish, shrimp and marinade in shallow dish, cover, refrigerate several hours or overnight.

Drain fish and shrimp, reserve marinade. Top sauteed leeks with fish and shrimp; drizzle with reserved marinade. Serve with seed crackers.

Marinade: Heat oil in skillet, add seeds, garlic and chili peppers, cook until fragrant. Add remaining ingredients, simmer, uncovered, 2 minutes; cool 10 minutes.

Sauteed Leeks: Cut leeks into 2½ inch thin strips. Heat butter in skillet, add leeks, cook, stirring, until just soft.

Seed Crackers: Sift flour into bowl, rub in butter, add egg and enough water to make ingredients cling together. Turn dough onto lightly floured surface, knead lightly until smooth. Divide dough into 4 portions, roll each portion out to ¹⁄₁₆ inch thick. Place on lightly greased baking sheets, brush with milk, sprinkle with combined salt, poppy and sesame seeds. Bake in 350°F oven about 10 minutes or until well browned. Cool on wire rack.
Serves 4.

WARM SALAD OF MUSSELS AND LEEK

4lb small mussels
3 cloves garlic, minced
½ cup dry white wine
½ cup chopped fresh parsley
1 small leek
2 teaspoons balsamic vinegar
1 cup firmly packed flat-leafed
parsley leaves, extra

TOMATO AND CUCUMBER SALSA
2 green cucumbers, peeled,
seeded, chopped
4 large tomatoes, peeled,
seeded, chopped
4 teaspoons sweet chili sauce
2 cloves garlic, minced
2 teaspoons grated fresh gingerroot
2 teaspoons balsamic vinegar

Scrub mussels, remove beards. Heat garlic, wine and parsley in large pan, add mussels, cook, covered, over high heat about 5 minutes or until mussels open; remove mussels from pan. Discard any unopened mussels. Return pan to heat, simmer, uncovered, until liquid is reduced to about ⅓ cup. Cut leek into rings, add leek and vinegar to pan, cook, stirring, until leek is just tender.

Remove and discard half of each mussel shell. Spoon warm leek mixture over mussels in shell, serve with extra parsley leaves and tomato and cucumber salsa.

Tomato and Cucumber Salsa: Combine all ingredients in bowl; mix well.

Serves 6.

LEFT: Chili Lime Seafood with Seed Crackers.
BELOW: Warm Salad of Mussels and Leek.

51

ULTIMATE SALAD SANDWICH

½ cup firmly packed fresh
    basil leaves
4 teaspoons pine nuts
3 tablespoons grated Parmesan
    cheese
3 tablespoons sour cream
8 slices wholegrain rye bread
2 hard-boiled eggs, sliced
1 cucumber, peeled, thinly sliced
1 carrot, finely grated
1 avocado, sliced
1½oz snow pea sprouts
1 cup (about 2oz) lentil sprouts
½ cup cottage cheese

Process basil and nuts until combined, add Parmesan cheese and cream, process until smooth. Spread basil mixture evenly over 4 slices of bread, top with egg slices, cucumber, carrot, avocado, snow pea sprouts, lentil sprouts and cottage cheese. Add remaining bread slices.

Makes 4.

MINTED BARLEY AND FRESH TOMATO SALAD

1 cup (7oz) barley
2 small green cucumbers,
    seeded, chopped
4 tomatoes, peeled, seeded,
    chopped
6 radishes, sliced
½ cup chopped fresh parsley
¼ cup chopped fresh mint
2 green onions, chopped
1 small bunch chicory

DRESSING
⅔ cup olive oil
¼ cup red wine vinegar
2 teaspoons dark brown sugar

Add barley to pan of boiling water, simmer, uncovered, until tender; drain, rinse under cold water, drain well. Combine barley, cucumbers, tomatoes, radishes, herbs, onions and dressing in bowl. Serve salad with chicory leaves.

Dressing: Combine all ingredients in screw-top jar; shake well.

Serves 2 to 4.

BLACK-EYED PEA SALAD WITH BAGEL CROUTONS

Peas best prepared a day ahead; store, covered, at room temperature.

2 cups (14oz) dried black-eyed peas
7oz small yellow pattypan
    squash, quartered
7oz small green pattypan
    squash, quartered
¾lb sugar snap peas

DRESSING
⅓ cup red wine vinegar
4 teaspoons Dijon mustard
2 teaspoons sugar
⅔ cup olive oil
2 cloves garlic, minced

BAGEL CROUTONS
4 bagels, thinly sliced
½ cup (1 stick) butter, melted
4 teaspoons chopped fresh parsley
4 teaspoons chopped fresh thyme
1 teaspoon chopped fresh oregano
½ teaspoon garlic powder

Place black-eyed peas in bowl, cover well with water, cover, stand overnight.

Drain peas, add to pan of boiling water, simmer, uncovered, until just tender; drain. Boil, steam or microwave squash and sugar snap peas separately until just tender. Drain, rinse under cold water, drain well. Combine black-eyed peas, squash, sugar snap peas and dressing in bowl; mix well. Serve with bagel croutons.

Dressing: Combine all ingredients in screw-top jar; shake well.

Bagel Croutons: Brush both sides of sliced bagels with combined butter, herbs and garlic powder. Place on baking sheets in single layer, bake in 350°F oven about 10 minutes or until crisp.

Serves 4 to 6.

NUTTY TOFU AND POTATO SALAD

3 new potatoes
½lb green beans, halved
¾lb package firm tofu, drained
oil for deep-frying
2 small bunches (about 1½lb)
    bok choy, chopped
1 cup (about 2½oz) bean sprouts
1 small green cucumber, chopped

PEANUT DRESSING
4 teaspoons salad oil
1 small onion, finely chopped
1½ teaspoons curry powder
½ teaspoon ground cumin
1½ teaspoons sweet chili sauce
2 teaspoons all-purpose flour
½ cup chunky peanut butter
⅔ cup vegetable broth
1⅔ cups canned unsweetened
    coconut milk
1 tablespoon dark brown sugar
¼ cup chopped unsalted
    roasted peanuts

Boil, steam or microwave potatoes and beans separately until tender; drain, rinse under cold water, drain well. Cut potatoes into quarters. Cut tofu into ¾ inch squares, pat dry on absorbent paper. Deep-fry tofu in batches in hot oil until lightly browned; drain on absorbent paper.

Combine potatoes, beans, tofu, bok choy, bean sprouts and cucumber in bowl; drizzle with hot peanut dressing.

Peanut Dressing: Heat oil in skillet, add onion, cook, stirring, until soft. Add curry powder, cumin, sauce and flour, cook, stirring, 2 minutes. Stir in remaining ingredients, stir over heat until mixture boils and thickens slightly.

Serves 4.

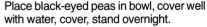

LEFT: Ultimate Salad Sandwich.
RIGHT: Clockwise from left: Minted Barley and Fresh Tomato Salad, Black-Eyed Pea Salad with Bagel Croutons, Nutty Tofu and Potato Salad.

RATATOUILLE SALAD

2 large red bell peppers
3 Italian eggplants
½ cup olive oil
3 egg tomatoes
1 large zucchini
3 tablespoons pine nuts, toasted
2 tablespoons shredded fresh basil
⅓ cup small black olives

TOMATO VINAIGRETTE
1 large tomato
2 teaspoons olive oil
1 teaspoon white vinegar
ground black pepper

Quarter peppers, remove seeds and membranes. Broil peppers, skin-side-up, until skin blisters and blackens. Peel away skin, cut peppers into thin strips. Thinly slice eggplants lengthways.

Heat oil in skillet, add eggplant in batches, cook until lightly browned; drain on absorbent paper. Slice tomatoes lengthways; discard seeds. Cut zucchini into 2 inch matchsticks. Pour tomato vinaigrette onto 4 plates, top with peppers, eggplants, tomatoes and zucchini, sprinkle with nuts, basil and olives.
Tomato Vinaigrette: Blend or process all ingredients until well combined, push through sieve; discard seeds.

Serves 2 to 4.

HERBED GARBANZO BEAN SALAD WITH PITA CRISPS

2 pita pocket breads
8¾oz can garbanzo beans,
    rinsed, drained
2 small green cucumbers,
    seeded, chopped
2 tomatoes, peeled, seeded, chopped
3 green onions, sliced
⅓ cup black olives, pitted, quartered
½ cup chopped fresh mint
½ cup chopped fresh cilantro
1 romaine lettuce, shredded
½ cup plain yogurt

DRESSING
½ cup olive oil
¼ cup fresh lemon juice
1 clove garlic, minced
1 teaspoon sugar

Split pocket breads in half, place in single layer on baking sheet, bake in 350°F oven 10 minutes, turn bread, continue cooking further 10 minutes or until lightly browned and dry. Break bread into pieces.

Combine beans, cucumbers, tomatoes, onions, herbs and lettuce in bowl, add dressing; mix well. Serve salad with yogurt and pita crisps.
Dressing: Combine all ingredients in screw-top jar; shake well.

Serves 4.

SAFFRON RICE AND NUTTY TOFU SALAD

3 tablespoons ghee
4 teaspoons grated fresh gingerroot
2 cloves garlic, minced
1 teaspoon sambal oelek
1 teaspoon coriander seeds, crushed
1 teaspoon cuminseed, crushed
½ teaspoon cardamom seeds
2 cinnamon sticks
1½ cups (10oz) basmati rice
3 cups boiling water
tiny pinch ground saffron
1 large vegetable bouillon cube
3 tablespoons ghee, extra
½ cup unsalted macadamias
½ cup whole blanched almonds
½ cup flaked coconut, toasted
4 teaspoons sugar

FRIED TOFU
10oz package firm tofu
all-purpose flour
oil for deep-frying

Heat ghee in pan, add gingerroot, garlic, sambal oelek, seeds and cinnamon sticks, cook, stirring, until fragrant. Add rice, water, saffron and crumbled bouillon cube, simmer, uncovered, until almost all liquid is evaporated. Cover, cook over low heat about 10 minutes, remove from heat, stand, covered, further 10 minutes. Discard cinnamon sticks.

Heat extra ghee in skillet, add nuts, cook, stirring, until browned. Combine rice, nut mixture, coconut, sugar and fried tofu in bowl; mix gently. Serve salad warm or cold.
Fried Tofu: Drain tofu on absorbent paper, cut into ½ inch cubes. Toss cubes in flour, shake away excess flour. Deep-fry tofu in hot oil until browned; drain on absorbent paper.

Serves 4.

RIGHT: Clockwise from left: Herbed Garbanzo Bean Salad with Pita Crisps, Saffron Rice and Nutty Tofu Salad, Ratatouille Salad.

FELAFEL ROLLS WITH HUMMUS AND SALAD

¾ cup dried broad beans (fava)
¾ cup dried garbanzo beans
1 small onion, chopped
2 cloves garlic, chopped
2 teaspoons ground coriander
1 teaspoon ground cumin
¼ teaspoon paprika
⅛ teaspoon cayenne pepper
3 tablespoons chopped fresh parsley
oil for deep-frying
6 large pita bread rounds
1 iceberg lettuce, shredded
2 tomatoes, sliced
2 small green cucumbers, sliced
1 red onion, sliced

HUMMUS
15oz can garbanzo beans, drained
2 cloves garlic, minced
⅓ cup fresh lemon juice
⅓ cup tahini (sesame paste)
4 teaspoons water

YOGURT DRESSING
1 cup plain yogurt
1 clove garlic, minced
3 tablespoons chopped fresh parsley

Place beans in bowl, cover well with cold water, cover, stand 48 hours, change water once. Place beans in bowl, cover well with cold water, cover, stand 15 hours.

Drain broad beans, peel and discard skins. Drain garbanzo beans. Process beans, onion and garlic until finely minced. Transfer mixture to bowl, stir in coriander, cumin, paprika, cayenne pepper and parsley. Roll 3 level tablespoons of mixture into balls, stand 30 minutes. Deep-fry felafel in hot oil until browned and cooked; drain on absorbent paper.

Heat pita bread in 350°F oven 5 minutes, spread with hummus, top with lettuce, tomatoes, cucumbers, onion and warm felafel. Drizzle with yogurt dressing, roll up firmly.

Hummus: Process all ingredients until smooth and creamy.

Yogurt Dressing: Combine all ingredients in bowl; mix well.

Serves 6.

BROCCOLI AND CAULIFLOWER WITH TAHINI DRESSING

1½lb broccoli, chopped
1½lb cauliflower, chopped
1 large red bell pepper, finely chopped
2½ cups (about 5oz) lentil sprouts

TAHINI DRESSING
⅓ cup tahini (sesame paste)
3 tablespoons fresh lemon juice
½ cup water
⅓ cup olive oil
1 teaspoon sugar
½ teaspoon garlic salt

Boil, steam or microwave broccoli and cauliflower until just tender; drain, rinse under cold water, drain well. Combine broccoli, cauliflower, pepper and sprouts in bowl; drizzle with tahini dressing.

Tahini Dressing: Blend or process tahini, juice and water until pale and thick; stir in remaining ingredients.

Serves 4.

FETA RAVIOLI WITH ARTICHOKES AND EGGPLANT

2 cups all-purpose flour
3 eggs
2 teaspoons olive oil

FILLING
5oz feta cheese
2oz packaged cream cheese
2 tablespoons sour cream
2 teaspoons chopped fresh thyme
2 teaspoons chopped fresh chives

DRESSING
3 tablespoons balsamic vinegar
½ cup olive oil
1 clove garlic, minced

ARTICHOKE AND EGGPLANT SALAD
2 red bell peppers
1 large eggplant, sliced
oil for deep-frying
12oz jar artichokes, drained
2 tomatoes, peeled, seeded, sliced
3 tablespoons chopped fresh oregano
½ cup firmly packed flat-leafed
    parsley leaves

Process flour, eggs and oil until combined. Turn onto lightly floured surface, knead until smooth. Cover, refrigerate 30 minutes. Divide dough into 4 pieces, roll 2 pieces separately until ¹⁄₁₆ inch thick.

Place teaspoons of filling 1½ inches apart over 1 sheet of pasta. Lightly brush second pasta sheet with water, place over filling, press firmly between filling. Cut into square ravioli shapes; lightly sprinkle with flour. Repeat with remaining dough and filling.

Add ravioli to large pan of boiling water, simmer, uncovered, about 2 minutes or until just tender; drain, rinse under cold water; drain. Toss ravioli in half the dressing, reserve remaining dressing for artichoke and eggplant salad. Serve ravioli with artichoke and eggplant salad.

Filling: Process cheeses, cream and herbs until just combined.
Dressing: Combine all ingredients in screw-top jar; shake well.
Artichoke and Eggplant Salad: Quarter peppers, remove seeds and membranes. Broil, skin-side-up, until skin blisters and blackens. Peel skin, slice peppers. Deep fry eggplant in hot oil until browned; drain. Combine peppers, eggplant, reserved dressing and remaining ingredients in bowl; mix well.

Serves 4 to 6.

POTATO BASKETS WITH CHILI BELL PEPPER DRESSING

3 large (about 1¼lb) potatoes, grated
4 teaspoons all-purpose flour
1 egg yolk
1 teaspoon seasoned pepper
⅓ cup light olive oil

VEGETABLE SALAD
7oz snow peas
2 carrots
4 cups (about 10oz) bean sprouts
4 teaspoons light soy sauce
½ teaspoon Oriental sesame oil

CHILI BELL PEPPER DRESSING
1 large red bell pepper
½ cup olive oil
¼ cup sweet chili sauce

Combine potatoes, flour, yolk and pepper in bowl; mix well. Heat 4 teaspoons of the oil in skillet, add quarter of the potato mixture, flatten to a 6½ inch round, cook until browned underneath, turn, cook until browned on other side. Repeat with remaining oil and potato mixture.

Press warm potato rounds over up-turned individual pie dishes on baking sheet. Bake in 375°F oven about 20 minutes or until potato baskets are firm; turn onto wire rack to cool. Serve potato baskets with vegetable salad and chili bell pepper dressing.

Vegetable Salad: Cut peas and carrots into thin strips of the same length. Combine vegetables, bean sprouts, sauce and oil in bowl; mix well.
Chili Bell Pepper Dressing: Quarter peppers, remove seeds and membranes. Broil peppers, skin-side-up, until skin blisters and blackens. Peel away skin, chop peppers. Blend or process peppers, oil and sauce until smooth.

Serves 4.

LEFT: From left: Felafel Rolls with Hummus and Salad, Broccoli and Cauliflower with Tahini Dressing.
RIGHT: From back: Potato Baskets with Chili Bell Pepper Dressing, Feta Ravioli with Artichokes and Eggplant.

TWICE-BAKED VEGETABLES AND RICE SALAD

3 tablespoons olive oil
1 red bell pepper, quartered
1 green bell pepper, quartered
6 Italian eggplants, halved
4 cloves garlic, halved
1 lemon
1 red onion, sliced
½ cup olive oil, extra
¼ cup fresh lemon juice
1 cup (7oz) brown rice
⅓ cup fresh mint leaves
⅓ cup fresh flat-leafed parsley leaves
1 small green cucumber, sliced

TAHINI SAUCE
⅔ cup fresh orange juice
4 teaspoons fresh lemon juice
⅓ cup tahini (sesame paste)

Combine oil, peppers, eggplants and garlic in roasting pan, stir until vegetables are coated with oil. Bake, covered, in 375°F oven 15 minutes, uncover, bake further 15 minutes or until vegetables are tender.

Using a vegetable peeler, cut peel thinly from lemon, avoiding any white pith; cut peel into fine strips. Combine vegetables, peel strips, onion, extra oil and juice in bowl, cover, refrigerate several hours.

Add rice to pan of boiling water, boil, uncovered, about 30 minutes or until just tender, drain.

Place vegetable mixture in roasting pan, bake, covered, in 375°F oven about 12 minutes or until heated through. Stir in herbs and cucumber. Serve vegetables warm or cold with rice and tahini sauce.

Tahini Sauce: Beat juices and tahini in small bowl until pale and thickened slightly.

Serves 4.

PICKLED BABY BEETS WITH HASH BROWNS

Beets best pickled a week ahead; store in sealed jar in a cool, dark cupboard.

12 (about 2lb) baby beets
¾ cup sugar
¾ cup red wine vinegar
½ cup white wine vinegar
¼ cup dry red wine
2 teaspoons black peppercorns
1 teaspoon yellow mustard seeds
4 sprigs lemon thyme

HASH BROWNS
2 tablespoons (¼ stick) butter
1 onion, finely chopped
1 clove garlic, minced
5 potatoes, grated
3 tablespoons Dijon mustard
1 tablespoon chopped fresh
    lemon thyme
1 teaspoon grated lemon zest
all-purpose flour
¼ cup light olive oil

MUSTARD CRESS DRESSING
⅓ cup olive oil
3 tablespoons fresh lemon juice
2 teaspoons yellow mustard seeds
½ teaspoon sugar
4 teaspoons mustard cress

Trim leaves about 1¼ inches from beets. Add unpeeled beets to large pan of boiling water, simmer, uncovered, about 40 minutes or until tender. Peel beets; pack into sterilized jar.

Combine sugar, vinegars, wine, peppercorns, yellow mustard seeds and thyme in pan, stir over heat, without boiling, until sugar is dissolved. Pour pickling liquid over beets to cover completely; seal while hot.

Remove beets from liquid, discard liquid. Cut beets into quarters, serve warm or cold with hash browns; drizzle with mustard cress dressing.

Hash Browns: Heat butter in skillet, add onion and garlic, cook, stirring, until onion is soft. Add potatoes, stir until potatoes are sticky, remove from heat, stir in mustard, thyme and zest. Shape mixture into 4 x 4 inch patties with wet hands. Toss patties in flour, shake away excess flour. Heat oil in skillet, add hash browns, cook about 10 minutes each side or until lightly browned and cooked through.

Mustard Cress Dressing: Combine all ingredients in screw-top jar; shake well.

Serves 4.

LEFT: From left: Twice-Baked Vegetables and Rice Salad, Pickled Baby Beets with Hash Browns.

CILANTRO TOFU SALAD WITH SPICY DRESSING

2 x ¾lb packages firm tofu
oil for deep-frying
12 sprigs fresh cilantro
½lb fresh asparagus spears,
chopped
2 carrots
½ small red onion, sliced
8 small radishes, sliced
1 cup (about 2½oz) bean sprouts
8oz can water chestnuts,
drained, halved
⅓ cup unsalted roasted peanuts

SPICY DRESSING
½ cup salad oil
⅓ cup fresh lime juice
3 tablespoons chopped fresh cilantro
4 teaspoons chopped fresh
lemon grass
1 small fresh red chili pepper,
finely chopped
4 teaspoons light soy sauce
1 tablespoon sugar
1 clove garlic, minced

Wrap tofu in 3 sheets of absorbent paper, weigh down with plate; stand 4 hours. Cut tofu into ¾ inch x 2 inch lengths. Deep-fry tofu in batches in hot oil until browned; drain on absorbent paper. Deep-fry cilantro in batches until bright green; drain on absorbent paper. Boil, steam or microwave asparagus until just tender; drain, rinse under cold water, drain. Cut carrot into long, thin strips. Combine all ingredients and spicy dressing in bowl; mix well.

Spicy Dressing: Combine all ingredients in screw-top jar; shake well.

Serves 4 to 6.

CORN GRIDDLE CAKES WITH SALSA AND GUACAMOLE

15oz canned whole-kernel corn
⅔ cup all-purpose flour
3 eggs

SALSA
2 limes
4 tomatoes, peeled, seeded,
thinly sliced
1 small red onion, thinly sliced
1 red bell pepper, thinly sliced
1 green bell pepper, thinly sliced
½ small fresh red chili pepper,
finely chopped
3 tablespoons chopped fresh cilantro
1 clove garlic, minced
3 tablespoons fresh lime juice
½ teaspoon sugar
3 tablespoons olive oil
4 teaspoons tomato puree

GUACAMOLE
1 large ripe avocado,
roughly chopped
1 clove garlic, minced
4 teaspoons fresh lime juice
½ small fresh red chili pepper,
seeded, finely chopped
3 tablespoons sour cream

Drain corn, reserve ⅓ cup corn. Process flour, eggs and remaining corn until smooth; stir in reserved corn. Pour heaped tablespoons of batter into heated greased griddle pan, cook until lightly browned underneath, turn, cook other side. Serve griddle cakes warm with salsa and guacamole.

Salsa: Using a vegetable peeler, cut peel thinly from limes, avoiding white pith; cut peel into thin strips. Combine zest, tomatoes, onion, peppers, chili pepper and cilantro in bowl. Add combined garlic, juice, sugar, oil and puree; mix well.

Guacamole: Process avocado, garlic, juice and chili until smooth, add sour cream, process until just combined.

Serves 4.

BELOW: From left: Cilantro Tofu Salad with Spicy Dressing, Corn Griddle Cakes with Salsa and Guacamole.
RIGHT: From left: Nutty Carrot, Currant and Bulgur Salad, Herb Gnocchi with Cauliflower and Almonds.

NUTTY CARROT, CURRANT AND BULGUR SALAD

⅓ cup bulgur
4 carrots, grated
½ cup dried currants
½ cup slivered almonds, toasted
⅓ cup chopped fresh cilantro

DRESSING
3 tablespoons olive oil
3 tablespoons fresh lime juice
1 teaspoon ground cumin
½ teaspoon ground cinnamon
½ teaspoon sugar

Place bulgur in bowl, cover with boiling water, stand 15 minutes; drain. Pat bulgur dry between layers of absorbent paper. Combine bulgur with remaining ingredients in bowl, add dressing; mix well.
Dressing: Combine all ingredients in screw-top jar; shake well.

Serves 2 to 4.

HERB GNOCCHI WITH CAULIFLOWER AND ALMONDS

10oz cauliflower, chopped
⅓ cup whole blanched almonds, toasted

HERB GNOCCHI
4 large (about 1½lb) old potatoes
1 egg, lightly beaten
¼ cup fine semolina
¼ cup chopped fresh basil
¼ cup chopped fresh chives
⅓ cup grated Parmesan cheese
1¼ cups all-purpose flour

TOMATO DRESSING
⅓ cup white wine vinegar
¾ cup salad oil
½ teaspoon sugar
2 teaspoons Dijon mustard
2 green onions, finely chopped
2 tomatoes, peeled, seeded, chopped

Boil, steam or microwave cauliflower until tender; drain, cool. Combine cauliflower, herb gnocchi and tomato dressing in bowl; mix gently, sprinkle with nuts.
Herb Gnocchi: Boil, steam or microwave potatoes until tender; drain. Push potatoes through sieve into large bowl. Stir in egg, semolina, herbs, cheese and enough flour to mix to a soft dough. Knead dough on floured surface until smooth. Shape level teaspoons of dough into balls. Place a ball in palm of hand, press floured fork onto ball of dough to make indentation and flatten slightly. Repeat with remaining balls.

Add gnocchi to large pan of boiling water, simmer, uncovered, about 3 minutes or until tender; drain, rinse under cold water, drain well.
Tomato Dressing: Combine all ingredients in bowl; mix well.

Serves 4.

BRAISED ARTICHOKE AND CAULIFLOWER SALAD

You will need a small piece of muslin for this recipe.

8 small fresh artichokes
⅔ cup olive oil
10 green onions, chopped
5oz button mushrooms, chopped
1 small green cucumber, chopped
4 stalks celery, chopped
1 bay leaf
10 black peppercorns
10 coriander seeds
3 tablespoons tomato paste
2 cloves garlic, minced
3 tablespoons fresh lemon juice
1⅓ cups dry white wine
½ cup water
2 tomatoes, chopped
4 teaspoons fresh chervil sprigs

CAULIFLOWER SALAD
⅓ cup olive oil
1 small cauliflower, chopped
2 cloves garlic, minced
½ cup dry white wine
½ cup water
4 teaspoons fresh lemon juice
2 sprigs fresh thyme
1 bay leaf
⅛ teaspoon ground saffron
10 coriander seeds

Trim base of artichokes so they sit flat. Remove tough outer leaves and trim remaining leaves with scissors.

Pull away inside leaves and coarse centers with a spoon.

Heat oil in pan, add artichokes, onions, mushrooms, cucumber and celery, cook, stirring, 5 minutes. Tie bay leaf, peppercorns and seeds in a small piece of muslin. Add muslin bag, paste, garlic, juice, wine and water to pan. Simmer, covered, about 45 minutes or until artichokes are tender. Discard muslin bag.

Spoon some of the vegetable mixture into artichokes, serve with remaining vegetable mixture and cauliflower salad; sprinkle with tomato and chervil. Serve warm or cold.

Cauliflower Salad: Heat oil in pan, add cauliflower, cook, covered, stirring occasionally, 4 minutes. Add remaining ingredients, simmer, uncovered, about 10 minutes or until liquid is evaporated. Discard thyme and bay leaf.

Serves 4.

SWEET CHILI NUT BALL SALAD

10oz canned white kidney beans (cannellini), rinsed, drained
1 cup (5oz) unsalted roasted cashews
¼ cup smooth peanut butter
1½ teaspoons sambal oelek
1 egg
3 tablespoons light soy sauce
1 teaspoon paprika
1 cup (2½oz) fresh bread crumbs
oil for deep-frying
½lb fresh asparagus spears
½ x ¾lb package thin egg noodles
½lb cherry tomatoes

SWEET CHILI SAUCE
⅓ cup sugar
4 teaspoons white vinegar
¼ cup water
2 teaspoons chopped fresh lemon grass
1 small fresh red chili pepper, sliced
1 tablespoon fresh lime juice
4 teaspoons fresh cilantro leaves

Blend or process beans, nuts, peanut butter, sambal oelek, egg, sauce, paprika and bread crumbs until smooth. Roll 2 level teaspoons of mixture into balls. Deep-fry nut balls in batches in hot oil until lightly browned and crisp; drain on absorbent paper.

Cut asparagus into 1½ inch lengths. Boil, steam or microwave asparagus until tender; drain, rinse under cold water, drain well. Add noodles to pan of boiling water, boil until tender, drain. Combine asparagus, noodles and tomatoes in bowl, top with nut balls; drizzle with sweet chili sauce.

Sweet Chili Sauce: Combine sugar, vinegar, water and lemon grass in pan, cook, stirring, until sugar is dissolved; simmer, uncovered, about 3 minutes or until sauce thickens slightly. Stir in chili pepper, juice and cilantro.

Serves 4.

RIGHT: From left: Braised Artichoke and Cauliflower Salad, Sweet Chili Nut Ball Salad.

GOLDEN SQUASH SHELLS WITH CURRIED SWEET POTATO

6 golden nugget squash
¼ cup light olive oil
3lb sweet potato
½lb broccoli, chopped
6 green onions, chopped
4 hard-boiled eggs, sliced
⅔ cup unsalted roasted cashews
½ cup sour cream

CURRY MAYONNAISE
8 egg yolks
¾ cup fresh lemon juice
1 tablespoon curry powder
2 teaspoons ground cumin
2 teaspoons ground coriander
2 teaspoons garam masala
2 teaspoons ground cardamom
2 cups light olive oil

Cut tops from squash, scoop out seeds; discard seeds. Stand squash in ovenproof dish, add enough boiling water to come ½ inch up sides of squash, replace tops of squash; brush with oil. Bake, covered, in 375°F oven about 45 minutes or until tender, remove squash from dish; cool.

Cut sweet potato into ¾ inch pieces, place on baking sheet. Bake, uncovered, in 400 F oven about 30 minutes or until just tender; cool. Boil, steam or microwave broccoli until just tender; drain, rinse under cold water, drain well.

Combine sweet potato, broccoli, onions, eggs, nuts and sour cream in bowl; stir in curry mayonnaise. Serve curried potato mixture in squash shells.
Curry Mayonnaise: Blend or process egg yolks, juice and spices until smooth. Gradually add oil in a thin stream while motor is operating, blend until thick.

Serves 6.

PEPPERED FETTUCCINE WITH TOMATOES AND BOCCONCINI

½lb fettuccine pasta
½lb spinach fettuccine pasta
1 small red onion, sliced
½lb bocconcini, chopped
3 tablespoons drained green peppercorns, rinsed
½lb cherry tomatoes, halved
⅓ cup chopped fresh basil
⅔ cup olive oil
⅓ cup white wine vinegar
1 clove garlic, minced
4 teaspoons shredded fresh basil

Add pasta to large pan of boiling water, boil, uncovered, until just tender; drain, rinse under cold water, drain well. Combine pasta, onion, bocconcini, peppercorns, tomatoes and chopped basil in large bowl. Add combined oil, vinegar and garlic; mix well. Sprinkle with shredded basil.

Serves 4.

MEXICAN SALAD ROLL-UPS

4 pieces lavash bread
½ small iceberg lettuce, shredded
4 hard-boiled eggs, sliced
2 tomatoes, chopped
1 small green bell pepper, chopped
1 small onion, sliced
1 cup (¼lb) grated cheddar cheese
¼ cup sour cream

BEAN SPREAD
4 teaspoons light olive oil
2 onions, finely chopped
4 teaspoons sambal oelek
27oz can red kidney beans, rinsed, drained, mashed

AVOCADO SPREAD
2 avocados, peeled, mashed
2 cloves garlic, minced
4 teaspoons fresh lemon juice
dash tabasco sauce

Spread each piece of bread evenly with bean spread and avocado spread, top with lettuce, eggs, tomatoes, pepper, onion, cheese and sour cream. Roll up firmly to enclose filling.
Bean Spread: Heat oil in skillet, add onions, cook, stirring, until soft. Add sambal oelek, cook, stirring, 1 minute. Add beans, stir until well combined; cool.
Avocado Spread: Combine all ingredients in bowl; mix well.

Serves 4.

RIGHT: Clockwise from left: Golden Squash Shells with Curried Sweet Potato, Mexican Salad Roll-Ups, Peppered Fettuccine with Tomatoes and Bocconcini.

DEEP-FRIED CREPE PARCELS WITH SALAD LEAVES

1 egg, lightly beaten
1 egg yolk
1½ teaspoons olive oil
½ cup all-purpose flour
¾ cup milk
all-purpose flour, extra
oil for deep-frying, extra
1 bunch (about ¼lb) arugula
2 cups (about 3½oz) firmly packed watercress sprigs

FILLING
1 small zucchini
1 carrot
2 teaspoons butter
2 cloves garlic, minced
2oz button mushrooms, quartered
1 cup (about 3½oz) mung beans
2oz snow peas, thinly sliced
½ cup grated cheddar cheese
½ cup roasted unsalted cashews, chopped

BATTER
3 eggs, lightly beaten
¼ cup all-purpose flour

DRESSING
2 tablespoons fresh lemon juice
3 tablespoons salad oil
4 teaspoons roasted unsalted cashews, chopped

Combine egg, egg yolk, oil and flour in bowl. Gradually add milk, beating well after each addition; beat until smooth, cover, stand 30 minutes.

Pour 3 tablespoons of batter into heated greased crepe pan, cook until browned underneath. Turn crepe, brown other side. Repeat with remaining batter. You will need 6 crepes.

Divide filling into 6 portions. Place 1 portion of filling onto center of crepe, fold in ends, roll up to enclose filling. Repeat with remaining crepes and filling. Carefully coat filled crepes in extra flour, shake away excess flour. Dip crepes into batter, deep-fry in hot extra oil until browned and crisp, drain on absorbent paper. Serve crepes sliced with arugula and watercress; drizzle with dressing.

Filling: Cut zucchini and carrot into matchsticks. Heat butter in skillet, add garlic and mushrooms, cook, stirring, until mushrooms are soft; cool. Combine mushroom mixture, zucchini, carrot and remaining ingredients in bowl; mix well.

Batter: Combine ingredients in bowl, beat until smooth.

Dressing: Combine all ingredients in screw-top jar; shake well.

Serves 6.

PICKLED VEGETABLES WITH DEEP-FRIED BOCCONCINI

Pickled vegetables can be made a week ahead; store, covered, in refrigerator.

1lb bocconcini
all-purpose flour
2 eggs, lightly beaten
2 cups (5oz) fresh bread crumbs
2 teaspoons seasoned pepper
oil for deep-frying
1 romaine lettuce
1 green oak leaf lettuce
⅓ cup olive oil

PICKLED VEGETABLES
1 carrot
1 small green cucumber
1 small onion
½ red bell pepper
½ yellow bell pepper
3½oz cauliflower, chopped
2oz broccoli, chopped
¼ teaspoon yellow mustard seeds
1 teaspoon dill seeds
½ teaspoon fennel seeds
1 teaspoon black peppercorns
¾ cup white wine vinegar
⅓ cup dry white wine
⅓ cup water
⅓ cup honey
4 teaspoons sugar

Slice bocconcini into ½ inch pieces. Toss bocconcini in flour, shake away excess flour, dip into eggs then combined bread crumbs and pepper. Deep-fry bocconcini in hot oil until lightly browned; drain on absorbent paper. Serve bocconcini with torn lettuce and pickled vegetables. Combine reserved pickling liquid (from pickled vegetables) and oil in screw-top jar; shake well, drizzle dressing over salad.

Pickled Vegetables: Cut carrot and cucumber into thin strips, slice onion. Cut peppers into ¾ inch squares. Boil, steam or microwave carrot, cauliflower and broccoli until just tender, rinse under cold water; drain well.

Combine seeds, peppercorns, vinegar, wine, water, honey and sugar in pan, simmer, uncovered, 5 minutes. Combine vegetables in bowl, pour over hot pickling liquid, mix well; cool, cover, refrigerate at least 2 days. Strain vegetables, reserve ⅓ cup pickling liquid for dressing.

Serves 6.

LEFT: Deep-Fried Crepe Parcels with Salad Leaves.
RIGHT: Pickled Vegetables with Deep-Fried Bocconcini.

JAPANESE EGG AND SUSHI RICE BASKETS

8 sheets nori seaweed
14oz raw tuna fillet, thinly sliced
1 small green cucumber, thinly sliced
1 avocado, sliced
3 tablespoons pink pickled gingerroot
1½oz salmon roe
wasabi paste

SUSHI RICE
4 cups (1¾lb) white short-grain rice
4½ cups water
1 strip konbu seaweed
½ cup rice vinegar
3 tablespoons sugar
2½ teaspoons salt

OMELET
1 tablespoon butter
2 eggs, beaten

SAUCE
¼ cup light soy sauce
3 tablespoons mirin
1 teaspoon dark brown sugar
1 tablespoon sesame seeds, toasted

Layer 2 sheets of nori seaweed together at an angle.

Press layered nori between 2 lightly oiled medium heatproof bowls, place bowls on baking sheet, bake in 350°F oven 5 minutes; cool.

Gently remove nori from between bowls, taking care to retain shape. Repeat layering and baking with remaining nori. Spoon sushi rice into nori baskets, top with omelet strips, tuna, cucumber, avocado, gingerroot, roe and wasabi to taste; drizzle with sauce.

Sushi Rice: Rinse rice under cold water until water becomes clear. Cover rice with water, stand 1 hour; drain well.

Combine rice, water and seaweed in pan, bring to boil, simmer, covered, over low heat 18 minutes. Remove pan from heat, stand, covered, further 10 minutes; remove and discard seaweed. Turn rice into glass bowl, cool slightly. Combine vinegar, sugar and salt in pan, stir over heat until sugar is dissolved. Stir vinegar mixture into rice; cool.

Omelet: Heat quarter of the butter in small omelet pan. Pour quarter of the eggs into pan, cook omelet until lightly browned underneath. Turn omelet, brown other side. Repeat 3 times more with remaining butter and eggs. Cool omelets, cut into ½ inch strips.

Sauce: Combine all ingredients in screw-top jar; shake well.

Serves 4.

GOUDA CHEESE AND RED SALAD PIZZA

11in frozen pizza base
½lb gouda cheese, chopped
4 teaspoons olive oil

RED SALAD
1 small radicchio lettuce, shredded
1 small red onion, sliced
1 small red bell pepper, sliced
1 tomato, sliced
1 teaspoon sambal oelek
3 tablespoons balsamic vinegar
3 tablespoons olive oil

Place pizza base on baking sheet, bake in 375°F oven about 20 minutes or until browned and crisp. Top pizza base with combined red salad and cheese, bake in 375°F oven about 10 minutes or until cheese is melted and topping warm; drizzle with oil.
Red Salad: Combine all ingredients in bowl; mix well. Stand salad 15 minutes, drain, discard dressing.

Serves 2.

POACHED EGGS ON SPINACH WITH ANCHOVY MAYONNAISE

½ small French bread stick
¾ cup grated Parmesan cheese
1 teaspoon olive oil
4 slices bacon, finely chopped
1½ bunches (about 2lb) spinach
4 eggs, poached

ANCHOVY MAYONNAISE
3 egg yolks
3 tablespoons fresh lemon juice
3 anchovy fillets
1 teaspoon French mustard
½ cup grapeseed oil
½ cup olive oil
3 tablespoons water

Cut bread into thin slices, place on baking sheet, sprinkle with cheese, bake in 375°F oven about 10 minutes or until browned and crisp. Heat oil in skillet, add bacon, cook until crisp; drain on absorbent paper.

Combine spinach, half the anchovy mayonnaise and half the bacon in bowl. Divide mixture between 4 plates, top with warm poached egg, drizzle with remaining anchovy mayonnaise, sprinkle with remaining bacon. Serve with croutons.
Anchovy Mayonnaise: Process yolks, juice, anchovies and mustard until smooth, slowly add combined oils in a thin stream while motor is operating; add water, process until smooth.

Serves 4.

SPICY ORZO SALAD WITH OMELET ROLLS

2 cups (15oz) orzo pasta
6 eggs
1½lb pumpkin squash
⅓ cup light olive oil
2 onions, sliced
1 clove garlic, minced
½ teaspoon ground cinnamon
1 teaspoon ground gingerroot
½ teaspoon ground coriander
1 teaspoon garam masala
⅛ teaspoon ground saffron
½ cup red lentils
1½ cups water
½lb mushrooms, sliced
1 green bell pepper, chopped
8 fresh dates, sliced

Add pasta to large pan of boiling water, boil, uncovered, until tender, drain.

Lightly beat 2 of the eggs, add to small greased omelet pan, cook until set; remove from pan. Repeat twice more with remaining eggs. Roll up omelets tightly, slice thinly.

Cut squash into ¾ inch pieces. Heat oil in pan, add onions, garlic and spices, cook, stirring, until onions are soft. Add squash, lentils, water, mushrooms and pepper, cook, uncovered, stirring occasionally, until vegetables are tender. Add pasta and dates, stir until well combined. Serve warm or cold with omelet rolls.

Serves 4.

FAR LEFT: From back: Gouda Cheese and Red Salad Pizza, Japanese Egg and Sushi Rice Baskets.
LEFT: From back: Spicy Orzo Salad with Omelet Rolls, Poached Eggs on Spinach with Anchovy Mayonnaise.

LAYERED ITALIAN SALAD

3 red bell peppers
1 eggplant
4 zucchini
1/3 cup olive oil
2 tablespoons (1/4 stick) butter
1lb button mushrooms, sliced
1 cup firmly packed fresh basil leaves
7oz mozzarella cheese, sliced
1 cup (5oz) black olives, pitted, halved
2 tomatoes, sliced

GARLIC DRESSING
1/2 cup olive oil
1/4 cup white wine vinegar
1 teaspoon sugar
2 cloves garlic, minced

Quarter peppers, remove seeds and membranes. Broil peppers, skin-side-up, until skin blisters and blackens; peel skin. Cut eggplant and zucchini lengthways into 1/4 inch slices. Place eggplant and zucchini on baking sheet, brush with oil, broil until well browned.

Heat butter in skillet, add mushrooms, cook, stirring, until moisture is evaporated.

Place eggplant over base of dish (6 cup capacity). Top with layer of peppers, basil, zucchini, cheese, olives, mushrooms and tomatoes; drizzle with garlic dressing. Cover, refrigerate salad several hours or overnight.

Garlic Dressing: Combine all ingredients in screw-top jar; shake well.

Serves 4.

CRISP FRIED POTATO SALAD

3lb small new potatoes
4 teaspoons light olive oil
4 teaspoons light olive oil, extra
2 onions, sliced
1/2lb sugar snap peas
1/2lb feta cheese
1 small red oak leaf lettuce

VINAIGRETTE
1/2 cup olive oil
1/4 cup white wine vinegar
2 teaspoons seeded mustard
1 clove garlic, minced
4 teaspoons chopped fresh chives

Boil, steam or microwave potatoes until tender; drain, cut potatoes in half. Heat oil on barbeque or in skillet, add potatoes, cook on cut side until browned and crisp; drain on absorbent paper. Heat extra oil in skillet, add onions, cook, stirring, until soft; drain on absorbent paper.

Boil, steam or microwave peas until just tender; drain, rinse under cold water, drain well. Cut cheese into small cubes. Combine potatoes, onions, peas and cheese in bowl, add vinaigrette; mix gently. Top lettuce leaves with potato mixture.

Vinaigrette: Combine all ingredients in screw-top jar; shake well.

Serves 4 to 6.

SMOKED TURKEY AND STILTON CHEESE SALAD

4 teaspoons light olive oil
1 red onion, sliced
1/2 teaspoon sugar
5oz sugar snap peas
1 small red leaf lettuce, shredded
1 small radicchio lettuce, shredded
5oz smoked turkey, chopped
5oz Stilton cheese, crumbled
6oz pumpernickel bread, chopped

DRESSING
2 1/2oz Stilton cheese, finely chopped
2/3 cup heavy cream
1/2 cup light sour cream
4 teaspoons cracked black
  peppercorns

Heat oil in skillet, add onion, cook, covered, stirring occasionally, until soft. Add sugar, stir until onions are lightly browned; drain on absorbent paper. Boil, steam or microwave peas until just tender; drain, rinse under cold water, drain well. Combine onion mixture, peas, torn lettuce leaves, turkey, cheese and bread in bowl; drizzle with dressing.

Dressing: Combine all ingredients in bowl; mix well.

Serves 4 to 6.

LEFT: Layered Italian Salad.
ABOVE: From back: Smoked Turkey and Stilton Cheese Salad, Crisp Fried Potato Salad.

BROILED GOATS' CHEESE ON RYE CROUTES

3/4lb goats' cheese
6 slices dark rye bread
2 teaspoons olive oil
2 Belgian endives
1 large bunch chicory
1 apple, sliced
1/3 cup hazelnuts, toasted, halved
3 tablespoons chopped fresh chives

THYME BUTTER
3 tablespoons butter
1 clove garlic, minced
2 teaspoons chopped fresh thyme
1/8 teaspoon cracked black
     peppercorns

HAZELNUT DRESSING
3 tablespoons red wine vinegar
1/4 cup olive oil
1/4 cup hazelnut oil

Cut cheese into 6 slices using a hot knife. Spread bread with thyme butter, place on baking sheet, bake in 375°F oven about 10 minutes or until underside of bread just starts to brown. Top croutes with cheese, brush with oil, broil until lightly browned and heated through.

Serve goats' cheese croutes with endive leaves, torn chicory leaves and apple, drizzle with hazelnut dressing, sprinkle with nuts and chives.
Thyme Butter: Blend or process all ingredients until well combined.
Hazelnut Dressing: Combine all ingredients in screw-top jar; shake well.

Serves 4 to 6.

CAESAR SALAD SANDWICH

1 teaspoon light olive oil
3 slices bacon, chopped
8 slices whole-wheat bread,
    toasted
3/4 cup walnuts, toasted, chopped
1 small romaine lettuce
4 hard-boiled eggs, sliced
1/4 cup Parmesan cheese flakes

ANCHOVY BUTTER
2 x 2oz cans anchovy fillets, drained
2 teaspoons Dijon mustard
3 tablespoons olive oil
3 tablespoons soft butter
2 cloves garlic, minced

DRESSING
1/2 teaspoon grated lemon zest
2 tablespoons fresh lemon juice
1 clove garlic, minced
1/3 cup olive oil

Heat oil in skillet, add bacon, cook until crisp; drain on absorbent paper. Spread each slice of toast with anchovy butter, sprinkle with nuts, press on firmly. Top 4 slices of toast with torn lettuce, egg slices, bacon and cheese; drizzle with dressing, cover with remaining toast.
Anchovy Butter: Blend or process all ingredients until well combined.
Dressing: Combine all ingredients in screw-top jar; shake well.

Serves 4.

WARM OKRA, EGG AND ROMANO CHEESE SALAD

8 eggs
2 tablespoons (1/4 stick) butter
1/2lb okra
5oz sugar snap peas
3 1/2oz piece romano cheese
1 red oak leaf lettuce
1 radicchio lettuce
3 cups (5oz) firmly packed
     watercress sprigs
1/2 cup (1 stick) butter, extra, melted
3 tablespoons balsamic vinegar

Place eggs in pan, cover with cold water. Bring to boil, stirring, then simmer, uncovered, 5 minutes. Drain, cover with cold water, stand 5 minutes. Peel eggs, cut into quarters lengthways.

Heat butter in skillet, add okra, cook, stirring, about 3 minutes or until just tender. Add peas, cook, stirring, until warm.

Using a vegetable peeler, cut flakes from cheese. Combine lettuce, watercress and cheese, top with warm okra mixture and eggs, drizzle with combined extra butter and vinegar.

Serves 4.

FAR LEFT: From back: Caesar Salad Sandwich, Broiled Goats' Cheese on Rye Croutes.
LEFT: Warm Okra, Egg and Romano Cheese Salad.

ACCOMPANIMENTS

You'll find a delicious range of accompaniments here. All the recipes are intended as side dishes which will transform the simplest meal into something special – whether it be a fresh salad made from a variety of leaves to dress up a humble broiled chop, or an interesting curried fruit salad to accompany roasted beef. Just mix and match to suit your tastes and the occasion. We have included rice, pasta, pulses and vegetables, plus green, leafy salads and a selection of unusual and appetizing fruit salads.

Most of the dressings can be made a day ahead, but the salads are best made just before serving.

TOASTED BARLEY TABBOULEH

¾ cup barley
1½ cups firmly packed flat-leafed
    parsley, chopped
¼ cup chopped fresh mint
½ small green cucumber, chopped
1 tomato, chopped
4 green onions, chopped
⅓ cup salad oil
3 tablespoons fresh lemon juice
1 clove garlic, minced

Place barley in dry skillet, stir over heat until lightly browned; remove from heat. Add barley to pan of boiling water, simmer, uncovered, about 25 minutes or until tender; drain well, cool. Combine barley with remaining ingredients in bowl; mix well.
Serves 6.

LEFT: Clockwise from left: New Potato, Corn and Bean Salad, White Kidney Bean, Egg and Salami Salad, Toasted Barley Tabbouleh.

WHITE KIDNEY BEAN, EGG AND SALAMI SALAD

1½oz sliced salami
19oz can white kidney beans
    (cannellini), rinsed, drained
1 tomato, peeled, seeded, chopped
1 small onion, finely chopped
⅓ cup shredded fresh basil
1 hard-boiled egg, finely grated
1 anchovy fillet, chopped

DRESSING
⅓ cup olive oil
3 tablespoons balsamic vinegar
½ teaspoon sugar

Cut salami into thin strips. Combine salami, beans, tomato, onion, basil and dressing in bowl; mix well. Top with egg and anchovy.
Dressing: Combine all ingredients in screw-top jar; shake well.
Serves 4 to 6.

NEW POTATO, CORN AND BEAN SALAD

2lb baby new potatoes, halved
17oz can whole-kernel corn,
    rinsed, drained
½ x 19oz can white kidney beans
    (cannellini), rinsed, drained
4 green onions, chopped
4 teaspoons chopped fresh chives

DRESSING
⅓ cup olive oil
3 tablespoons fresh lemon juice
½ cup mayonnaise
½ cup sour cream
1 teaspoon sugar
4 teaspoons Dijon mustard

Boil, steam or microwave potatoes until tender; drain, cool. Combine potatoes with remaining ingredients in bowl, add dressing; mix well.
Dressing: Combine all ingredients in bowl; whisk until smooth.
Serves 4 to 6.

PASTA WITH BEANS AND TANGY ONION RELISH

5oz penne pasta
5oz green beans

ONION RELISH
3 tablespoons light olive oil
1 large red onion, sliced
⅓ cup white wine vinegar
⅓ cup dry red wine
⅓ cup dark brown sugar

Add pasta to large pan of boiling water, boil, uncovered, until just tender; drain. Slice beans, boil, steam or microwave beans until just tender; drain, rinse under cold water, drain well. Combine pasta, beans and onion relish in bowl; mix lightly.
Onion Relish: Heat oil in pan, add onion, cook, stirring, until onion is soft. Add remaining ingredients, simmer, uncovered, 10 minutes, cool.

Serves 6.

MINTED COUSCOUS WITH PEAS AND MUSTARD SEEDS

2 teaspoons olive oil
2 teaspoons black mustard seeds
3 tablespoons butter
2¼ cups vegetable broth
1½ cups (9oz) couscous
1 cup (¼lb) cooked green peas
4 green onions, chopped

MINT DRESSING
½ cup salad oil
½ cup cider vinegar
1 teaspoon sugar
¼ cup chopped fresh mint

Heat oil in pan, add seeds, cook, covered, until seeds start to pop. Add butter and broth, bring to boil. Stir in couscous, return to boil, remove pan from heat. Cover pan, stand about 5 minutes or until liquid is absorbed. Separate grains with fork, spread onto tray; cool at room temperature. Combine couscous, peas, onions and mint dressing in bowl; mix lightly.
Mint Dressing: Combine all ingredients in screw-top jar; shake well.

Serves 6.

COUSCOUS, BELL PEPPER AND ROASTED GARLIC SALAD

2 red bell peppers
12 cloves garlic, peeled
⅓ cup olive oil
1½ cups chicken broth
2 cups (6oz) couscous
3oz (¾ stick) butter, melted

DRESSING
½ cup tomato juice
4 teaspoons balsamic vinegar
1½ teaspoons harissa
¼ cup olive oil
3 tablespoons chopped fresh marjoram
3 tablespoons chopped fresh chives

Quarter peppers, remove seeds and membranes. Broil peppers, skin-side-up, until skin blisters and blackens. Peel away skin, slice peppers finely.

Place garlic in small ovenproof dish, pour oil over garlic, bake, uncovered, in 350°F oven 25 minutes or until garlic is lightly browned and tender.

Bring broth to boil in pan, stir in couscous, remove from heat, stand

about 2 minutes or until liquid is absorbed. Add butter, stir over heat until couscous is coated. Spread couscous on tray, cool at room temperature. Combine couscous, peppers, roasted garlic and dressing in bowl; mix well.

Dressing: Combine all ingredients in screw-top jar; shake well.

Serves 4 to 6.

SESAME NOODLES WITH TANGY CITRUS SHREDS

**¾lb fresh egg noodles
4 teaspoons Oriental sesame oil
4 teaspoons olive oil
2 oranges
2 limes
1 lemon**

DRESSING
**½ cup fresh orange juice
¼ cup fresh lime juice
3 tablespoons fresh lemon juice
3 tablespoons peanut butter
1 teaspoon sambal oelek
4 teaspoons sugar
3 tablespoons cider vinegar
4 teaspoons Oriental sesame oil
4 teaspoons salad oil**

Add noodles to large pan of boiling water, boil, uncovered until just tender; drain, rinse under cold water, drain well. Place noodles in bowl, toss with combined oils.

Using vegetable peeler, cut peel thinly from oranges, limes and lemon, avoiding any white pith; cut peel into thin shreds. Place peel in pan, cover with cold water, bring to boil; drain, rinse under cold water; drain. Combine noodle mixture, peel and dressing in bowl; mix well.

Dressing: Blend or process all ingredients until smooth.

Serves 4 to 6.

LEFT: From left: Minted Couscous with Peas and Mustard Seeds, Pasta with Beans and Tangy Onion Relish.
RIGHT: From left: Couscous, Bell Pepper and Roasted Garlic Salad, Sesame Noodles with Tangy Citrus Shreds.

THAI SALAD WITH CRUNCHY RICE SQUARES

⅓ bunch (about 9oz) bok choy, chopped
1 yellow bell pepper, thinly sliced
1 red bell pepper, thinly sliced
1¼ cups (about ¼lb) mung bean sprouts
2 cups (about 5oz) bean sprouts
3 tablespoons shredded fresh basil

COCONUT CREAM DRESSING
½ cup canned unsweetened coconut cream
3 tablespoons fresh lime juice
½ teaspoon Oriental sesame oil
½ teaspoon honey
½ teaspoon fish sauce

RICE SQUARES
1 cup (7oz) white short-grain rice
2 cups chicken broth
4 teaspoons chopped fresh basil
½ teaspoon sambal oelek
oil for deep-frying

Combine bok choy, peppers, sprouts and basil in bowl; stir in coconut cream dressing, top with rice squares.
Coconut Cream Dressing: Combine all ingredients in screw-top jar; shake well.
Rice Squares: Grease deep 6 inch square baking pan, line base and sides with foil, grease foil. Combine rice and broth in pan, bring to boil, simmer, covered with tight-fitting lid, about 12 minutes or until liquid is absorbed and rice is sticky. Stir in basil and sambal oelek. Press mixture firmly into prepared pan, smooth top. Cover with greased foil, place another pan on top, weight down with heavy cans. Refrigerate rice several hours or overnight.

Remove rice mixture from pan, cut into ¾ inch squares. Deep-fry rice squares in batches in hot oil until lightly browned and crisp; drain on absorbent paper.

Serves 4 to 6.

BLACK BEAN AND BELL PEPPER SALAD

Black beans are also known as turtle beans. Beans best prepared a day ahead.

2½ cups (1lb) dried black beans
1 ham bone
1 small onion, halved
1 stalk celery, halved
1 carrot, halved
1 tablespoon cuminseed
2 red bell peppers, finely chopped
2 yellow bell peppers, finely chopped
⅓ cup chopped fresh cilantro
⅓ cup chopped fresh parsley

DRESSING
½ cup fresh lemon juice
½ cup olive oil
2 teaspoons Dijon mustard
1 clove garlic, minced
½ teaspoon sugar
1 teaspoon sambal oelek

Place beans in bowl, cover well with water, cover, stand overnight.

Drain beans, discard water. Combine beans, ham bone, onion, celery and carrot in large pan, add enough water to cover mixture. Bring to boil, simmer, covered, about 1 hour or until beans are tender. Drain beans; cool. Discard water, bone and vegetables.

Place seeds in dry pan, stir over gentle heat until fragrant; cool. Combine beans, seeds, peppers and herbs in bowl, add dressing; mix well.
Dressing: Combine all ingredients in screw-top jar: shake well.

Serves 6.

HERBED POTATO AND PASTA SALAD

½lb rigatoni pasta
2 large red-skinned potatoes
3 tablespoons olive oil
2 cloves garlic, minced
1 bunch (about 1¼lb) spinach
1 radicchio lettuce
2 green onions, chopped
¼ cup shredded fresh basil

DRESSING
3 tablespoons red wine vinegar
½ cup olive oil
4 teaspoons Dijon mustard
1 tablespoon dark brown sugar

Add pasta to large pan of boiling water, boil, uncovered, until just tender; drain, rinse under cold water, drain well.

Chop potatoes into ¾ inch pieces. Boil, steam or microwave potatoes until tender; drain, rinse under cold water, drain well. Heat oil in skillet, add garlic, spinach and torn lettuce leaves, cook, stirring, until spinach is just wilted. Combine pasta, potatoes, spinach mixture, onions, basil and dressing in bowl; mix well. Serve warm or cold.
Dressing: Combine all ingredients in screw-top jar; shake well.

Serves 6.

LEFT: Thai Salad with Crunchy Rice Squares.
RIGHT: From left: Black Bean and Bell Pepper Salad, Herbed Potato and Pasta Salad.

THREE BEAN, TOMATO AND EGGPLANT SALAD

⅓ cup dried red beans
⅓ cup dried black-eyed peas
1½ cups (6oz) frozen broad beans (fava), thawed
1 large eggplant
3 tablespoons olive oil
2 tomatoes, seeded, chopped
1 red onion, sliced

DRESSING
3 tablespoons balsamic vinegar
¼ cup olive oil
½ teaspoon grated lemon zest
3 tablespoons chopped fresh mint

Place red beans and black-eyed peas in large bowl, cover well with water, cover, stand overnight.

Drain beans, add to pan of boiling water, boil, uncovered, about 25 minutes or until tender; drain. Boil, steam or microwave broad beans until tender, remove outer skins.

Cut eggplant into ¾ inch pieces. Place eggplant in bowl, toss with oil. Place eggplant in single layer on baking sheet, bake, uncovered, in 400°F oven 20 minutes, turning occasionally; cool. Combine all beans, eggplant, tomatoes and onion in bowl, add dressing; mix well.
Dressing: Combine all ingredients in screw-top jar; shake well.

Serves 4.

CURRIED BROWN RICE AND CASHEW SALAD

2 cups (14oz) brown rice
3 tablespoons light olive oil
1 onion, finely chopped
2 cloves garlic, minced
2 teaspoons curry powder
2 teaspoons black mustard seeds
¾ cup golden raisins
¾ cup unsalted roasted cashews, chopped
2 carrots, grated
½ small red bell pepper, chopped
2 apples, peeled, grated
3 green onions, chopped
¼ cup chopped fresh parsley

DRESSING
1 egg yolk
3 tablespoons cider vinegar
⅓ cup salad oil
1 tablespoon curry powder

Add rice gradually to pan of boiling water, boil, uncovered, about 30 minutes or until tender; drain, cool.

Heat oil in skillet, add onion, garlic, curry powder and seeds, cook, stirring, until onion is soft; cool. Combine rice, onion mixture, raisins, nuts, carrots, pepper, apples, green onions and half the parsley in bowl, add dressing; mix well. Sprinkle with remaining parsley.
Dressing: Blend or process all ingredients until smooth.

Serves 8.

CURRIED PASTA AND RADISH SALAD

3 cups (½lb) shell pasta
4 green onions, chopped
10 radishes, sliced

CURRIED MAYONNAISE
4 teaspoons salad oil
4 teaspoons curry powder
4 teaspoons seeded mustard
4 teaspoons chopped fresh chives
½ cup grated cheddar cheese
1½ cups mayonnaise
3 tablespoons milk

Add pasta to large pan of boiling water, boil, uncovered, until just tender; drain, rinse under cold water, drain well. Combine pasta, onions and radishes in bowl, add curried mayonnaise; mix well.
Curried Mayonnaise: Heat oil in skillet, add curry powder, cook, stirring, until fragrant; cool. Combine curry mixture with remaining ingredients in bowl; mix well.

Serves 4 to 6.

MINTED RICE WITH FETA CHEESE

⅓ cup olive oil
1 onion, finely chopped
2 cups (14oz) white long-grain rice
3 cups chicken broth
5oz feta cheese, crumbled
½ cup chopped fresh mint

Heat oil in pan, add onion, cook, stirring, until soft. Add rice gradually, cook, stirring, 1 minute. Add broth, bring to boil, cook, covered, over low heat about 20 minutes or until liquid is absorbed and rice is tender. Remove pan from heat, stir in cheese and mint; cool. Spoon rice into 6 lightly oiled molds (1 cup capacity), cover, refrigerate several hours or overnight. Turn out to serve.

Serves 6.

LEFT: From left: Three Bean, Tomato and Eggplant Salad, Curried Brown Rice and Cashew Salad.
RIGHT: From top: Curried Pasta and Radish Salad, Minted Rice with Feta Cheese.

SPICY RICE WITH CRISP ONION AND COCONUT

1/8 teaspoon ground saffron
2 star anise
1 cinnamon stick
3 cardamom pods, crushed
2 1/2 cups (1lb) basmati rice
1/4 cup slivered almonds, toasted
1/2 cup flaked coconut, toasted
4 green onions, chopped
1 small onion, thinly sliced
oil for deep-frying

COCONUT DRESSING
1 2/3 cups canned unsweetened
   coconut cream
3 tablespoons fresh lime juice
1 teaspoon sugar
1/2 teaspoon garam masala

Add saffron, star anise, cinnamon and cardamom to large pan of cold water, bring to boil, add rice gradually, boil, uncovered, until tender; drain. Discard star anise and cinnamon stick, rinse rice under cold water; drain well. Combine rice, nuts, coconut, green onions and coconut dressing in bowl; mix well.

Deep-fry onion in hot oil until lightly browned; drain on absorbent paper. Sprinkle onion over salad.
Coconut Dressing: Combine all ingredients in bowl; mix well.

Serves 4 to 6.

CRUNCHY TOMATO AND FETTUCCINE SALAD

1/2lb spinach fettuccine pasta
3 slices whole-wheat bread
2 cloves garlic, minced
4 teaspoons olive oil
1/2lb cherry tomatoes, halved
1/3 cup shredded fresh basil
1/3 cup Parmesan cheese flakes

DRESSING
1 cup firmly packed fresh basil leaves
2 cloves garlic, minced
1/3 cup drained chopped sun-dried
   tomatoes
1/2 cup olive oil
1/4 cup balsamic vinegar
1 teaspoon sugar
1/4 teaspoon dried chili flakes

Add pasta to large pan of boiling water, boil, uncovered, until just tender; drain, rinse under cold water, drain well.

Process bread until finely crumbed, add garlic, process until combined. Heat oil in skillet, add bread crumb mixture, stir over heat until bread crumbs are browned and crisp. Combine pasta, tomatoes, basil and dressing in bowl; mix well. Sprinkle with bread crumbs and cheese.
Dressing: Blend or process all ingredients until combined.

Serves 6.

CHERRY TOMATO AND SPINACH RAVIOLI SALAD

1lb spinach and ricotta ravioli
7oz snow peas
1 red bell pepper, sliced
1/2lb cherry tomatoes
4 green onions, chopped
1/2 red onion, sliced

CREAMY HERB DRESSING
1/3 cup olive oil
3 tablespoons white wine vinegar
1/2 cup sour cream
1 clove garlic, minced
4 teaspoons chopped fresh chives
2 teaspoons chopped fresh thyme
2 teaspoons chopped fresh rosemary
2 teaspoons chopped fresh basil

Add pasta to large pan of boiling water, boil, uncovered, until just tender; drain, cool. Boil, steam or microwave snow peas until just tender; drain, rinse under cold water, drain well.

Combine pasta, snow peas, pepper, tomatoes, green onions and onion in bowl; add creamy herb dressing.
Creamy Herb Dressing: Combine all ingredients in screw-top jar; shake well.

Serves 8.

CRACKED WHEAT AND RICE SALAD

1/2 cup bulgur
1 1/4 cups (1/2lb) white rice
1/2 cup wild rice
15oz can baby corn, drained
4 green onions, chopped

DRESSING
3 tablespoons light soy sauce
1/4 teaspoon Oriental sesame oil
3 tablespoons honey
1/3 cup salad oil
1 clove garlic, minced

Place bulgur in bowl, cover with boiling water, stand 15 minutes. Rinse bulgur, drain, pat dry with absorbent paper. Add rices gradually to separate pans of boiling water, boil, uncovered, until just tender; drain, rinse under cold water, drain well.

Combine bulgur, rices, corn and onions in bowl. Add dressing, mix gently; cover, refrigerate 1 hour.
Dressing: Combine all ingredients in screw-top jar; shake well.

Serves 6.

LEFT: From left: Crunchy Tomato and Fettuccine Salad, Spicy Rice with Crisp Onion and Coconut.
RIGHT: From back: Cracked Wheat and Rice Salad, Cherry Tomato and Spinach Ravioli Salad.

DEEP-FRIED PASTA SALAD

2 cups (5oz) bow-tie pasta
all-purpose flour
3 eggs, lightly beaten
¼ cup milk
2½ cups (6oz) fresh bread crumbs
1 cup (2½oz) grated Parmesan
    cheese
oil for deep-frying

HERB DRESSING
¼ cup fresh lemon juice
¼ cup bottled Italian dressing
2 cups olive oil
4 teaspoons chopped fresh mint
4 teaspoons chopped fresh thyme
4 teaspoons chopped fresh rosemary

Add pasta to large pan of boiling water, boil, uncovered, until tender; drain, pat dry on absorbent paper. Toss pasta in flour, shake away excess flour. Dip pasta in combined eggs and milk, toss in combined bread crumbs and cheese. Cover pasta, refrigerate 1 hour.

Deep-fry pasta in batches in hot oil until lightly browned and crisp; drain on absorbent paper. Serve pasta hot or cold; drizzle with herb dressing.
Herb Dressing: Combine all ingredients in screw-top jar; shake well.
Serves 4.

FRUITY RICE AND CASHEW SALAD

2 cups (14oz) brown rice
½ cup chopped dried pears
½ cup chopped dried apricots
¼ cup chopped dried peaches
½ cup golden raisins
½ cup unsalted roasted cashews
4 green onions, chopped

DRESSING
4 teaspoons grated fresh gingerroot
3 tablespoons chopped fresh mint
1 cup apricot nectar
¼ teaspoon ground cardamom
4 teaspoons fresh lemon juice

Add rice gradually to large pan of boiling water, boil, uncovered, about 30 minutes or until tender; drain, rinse under cold water, drain well.

Combine rice, fruit, nuts and onions in bowl, add dressing; mix well.
Dressing: Combine all ingredients in screw-top jar; shake well.
Serves 4 to 6.

WILD RICE AND BARLEY SALAD WITH PISTACHIOS

1/4 cup wild rice
1/2 cup pearl barley
1 lime
1 grapefruit
1/2 cup unsalted pistachios, toasted
3 tablespoons sesame seeds, toasted
3 tablespoons pumpkin seed kernels
3 tablespoons sunflower seed kernels
5 dried pears, sliced
6 prunes, sliced
4 teaspoons fresh lime juice
2 teaspoons honey
1/2 teaspoon Oriental sesame oil

*LEFT: From back: Fruity Rice and Cashew
Salad, Deep-Fried Pasta Salad.
ABOVE: From left: Wild Rice and Barley
Salad with Pistachios, Caesar Pasta Salad.*

Add rice and barley gradually to pan of boiling water, boil, uncovered, stirring occasionally, about 30 minutes or until tender; drain, rinse under cold water, drain.

Using vegetable peeler, cut peel thinly from lime and grapefruit, avoiding any white pith. Cut peel into thin strips. Add peel to pan of boiling water, boil 1 minute; drain, rinse under cold water, drain. Combine rice, barley, peel, segmented grapefruit and remaining ingredients in bowl; mix well.

Serves 2 to 4.

CAESAR PASTA SALAD

1/2lb pasta twists
1 teaspoon olive oil
1 romaine lettuce
2oz can anchovy fillets, drained, chopped
1/2 cup Parmesan cheese flakes

DRESSING
6 green onions, chopped
3 cloves garlic, minced
1/2 cup olive oil
3 tablespoons fresh lemon juice
1 egg white
1 teaspoon Dijon mustard

GARLIC CROUTONS
1 small French bread stick
3 tablespoons butter, melted
2 cloves garlic, minced

Add pasta to large pan of boiling water, boil, uncovered, until just tender; drain, rinse under cold water, drain well. Place pasta in bowl; toss with oil.

Combine torn lettuce leaves, pasta, anchovies and half the cheese in bowl, add dressing; mix well. Add garlic croutons, sprinkle with remaining cheese.
Dressing: Blend or process all ingredients until well combined.
Garlic Croutons: Cut bread into 3/4 inch slices, cut slices into quarters. Toss bread in combined butter and garlic. Bake croutons on baking sheet in 350°F oven about 15 minutes or until crisp.

Serves 4.

PASTA WITH MANGOES AND RAISINS

½lb mafalde pasta
4 teaspoons olive oil
¼ teaspoon ground cloves
¼ teaspoon ground cardamom
¼ teaspoon ground cumin
1 teaspoon paprika
1 onion, chopped
2 cloves garlic, minced
2 small mangoes, chopped
⅔ cup dark seedless raisins
3 tablespoons chopped fresh chives
¼ cup chopped fresh parsley
⅓ cup olive oil, extra
4 teaspoons white wine vinegar

Add pasta to large pan of boiling water, boil, uncovered, until just tender; drain, rinse under cold water, drain well.

Heat oil in pan, add spices, onion and garlic, cook, stirring, until onion is soft, cool. Combine pasta, onion mixture and remaining ingredients in bowl; mix well.

Serves 6.

LENTIL SALAD WITH BLUE CHEESE DRESSING

1 small green bell pepper
1 small red bell pepper
1 large carrot
½ small leek
½ cup red lentils
½ cup brown lentils
15 slices hot salami

BLUE CHEESE DRESSING
1oz blue cheese
½ cup whipping cream
2 teaspoons sour cream
1 teaspoon fresh lemon juice
2 teaspoons chopped fresh dill

Remove seeds and membranes from peppers. Cut peppers, carrot and leek into very thin strips about the same size. Place vegetables in bowl, cover with iced water, stand about 20 minutes or until vegetables curl slightly; drain well.

Add red lentils to pan of boiling water, simmer, uncovered, about 8 minutes or until tender; drain, cool.

Add brown lentils to pan of boiling water, simmer, uncovered, about 20 minutes or until tender; drain, cool.

Cut salami into thin strips. Combine vegetables, lentils and salami in bowl; top with blue cheese dressing.

Blue Cheese Dressing: Combine crumbled cheese with remaining ingredients in bowl; beat until well combined.

Serves 4 to 6.

PROSCIUTTO AND BEAN SALAD WITH CHIVE DRESSING

3½oz sliced prosciutto
1 bunch chicory
1 romaine lettuce
19oz can white kidney beans (cannellini), rinsed, drained

CHIVE DRESSING
¼ cup sherry wine vinegar
1 teaspoon Dijon mustard
½ cup olive oil
2 teaspoons sugar
3 tablespoons chopped fresh chives

Cut prosciutto into thin strips, combine with torn chicory and lettuce leaves and beans in bowl; drizzle with chive dressing.

Chive Dressing: Combine all ingredients in screw-top jar; shake well.

Serves 4 to 6.

CILANTRO, LENTIL AND VEGETABLE SALAD

⅔ cup red lentils
1 carrot
1 small red bell pepper
1 cup (about 2½oz) shredded Chinese cabbage
4 cups (about 10oz) bean sprouts

CILANTRO DRESSING
1 cup firmly packed cilantro leaves
2 cloves garlic, minced
½ teaspoon sambal oelek
⅔ cup olive oil
4 teaspoons light soy sauce

Add lentils to pan of boiling water, simmer, uncovered, about 8 minutes or until lentils are just tender; drain, rinse under cold water, drain well. Cut carrot and pepper into very thin matchsticks.

Combine lentils, carrot, pepper, cabbage and sprouts in bowl; mix well, top with cilantro dressing.

Cilantro Dressing: Blend or process all ingredients until smooth.

Serves 6.

LEFT: From top: Lentil Salad with Blue Cheese Dressing, Pasta with Mangoes and Raisins.
RIGHT: From back: Cilantro, Lentil and Vegetable Salad, Prosciutto and Bean Salad with Chive Dressing.

SWEET POTATO AND GARBANZO BEAN SALAD

10oz sweet potato
10oz white sweet potato
⅓ cup light olive oil
2 tablespoons (¼ stick) butter
1 onion, chopped
¼ teaspoon chili powder
¼ teaspoon ground cinnamon
1 cup (¼lb) cooked green peas
10oz canned garbanzo beans, rinsed, drained

Cut sweet potatoes into 1¼ inch pieces. Heat oil and butter in skillet, add onion, cook, stirring, until soft. Add potatoes, cook slowly, covered, stirring occasionally, until vegetables are tender. Add spices, peas and beans, cook, stirring, until heated through. Serve warm or cold.

Serves 4.

CORN AND BLACK-EYED PEA SALAD

1 cup (7oz) dried black-eyed peas
2 green bell peppers
4 teaspoons cuminseed
17oz can whole-kernel corn, rinsed, drained
½lb cherry tomatoes
4 green onions, chopped
3 tablespoons chopped fresh cilantro

DRESSING
¼ cup sherry wine vinegar
½ cup olive oil
2 teaspoons sugar

Place peas in bowl, cover with boiling water, stand 1 hour. Drain peas, add to pan of boiling water, simmer, partly covered, about 30 minutes or until tender; drain, rinse under cold water, drain well.

Quarter peppers, remove seeds and membranes. Broil peppers, skin-side-up, on baking sheet until skin blisters and blackens. Peel away skin, cut peppers into strips. Add seeds to dry pan, stir over heat until fragrant. Combine peas, peppers, seeds, corn, tomatoes, onions and cilantro in bowl; add dressing, mix gently. Refrigerate until cold.

Dressing: Combine all ingredients in screw-top jar; shake well.

Serves 6.

BELOW: From left: Sweet Potato and Garbanzo Bean Salad, Corn and Black-Eyed Pea Salad.
RIGHT: From left: Pumpkin Squash, Rice and Seed Salad, Curried Garbanzo Bean Salad.

PUMPKIN SQUASH, RICE AND SEED SALAD

1 cup (7oz) white rice
3 green onions, chopped
¼ cup sesame seeds, toasted
¼ cup sunflower seed kernels
¼ cup pumpkin seed kernels
3½oz uncooked pumpkin squash, coarsely grated

DRESSING
3 tablespoons white wine vinegar
3 tablespoons honey
4 teaspoons light soy sauce
½ cup salad oil
3 tablespoons green ginger wine
⅛ teaspoon ground saffron

Add rice gradually to pan of boiling water, boil, uncovered, until tender; drain, rinse under cold water, drain well. Combine rice with remaining ingredients in bowl, add dressing; mix well.

Dressing: Combine all ingredients in screw-top jar; shake well.

Serves 4.

CURRIED GARBANZO BEAN SALAD

2 x 15oz cans garbanzo beans, rinsed, drained
1 small red onion, finely chopped
1 large mango, finely chopped
1 apple, peeled, chopped
4 teaspoons chopped fresh mint
4 teaspoons chopped fresh cilantro
¼ cup shredded coconut, toasted

DRESSING
¾ cup plain yogurt
1 tablespoon mango chutney
1 clove garlic, minced
2 teaspoons curry powder
4 teaspoons fresh lime juice

Combine all ingredients and dressing in bowl; mix well.

Dressing: Combine all ingredients in bowl; mix well.

Serves 4 to 6.

EGGPLANT, TOMATO AND ZUCCHINI STACKS

1 large (about 1lb) eggplant
oil for deep-frying
2 zucchini, thinly sliced
1 yellow bell pepper
2 large tomatoes

PESTO
1 cup firmly packed fresh basil leaves
1 clove garlic, minced
¼ cup pine nuts, toasted
⅓ cup olive oil
¼ cup grated Parmesan cheese

DRESSING
½ cup olive oil
4 teaspoons balsamic vinegar
¼ teaspoon sugar
1 clove garlic, minced

Cut eggplant into 12 x ½ inch slices. Deep-fry eggplant in batches in hot oil until lightly browned; drain on absorbent paper. Deep-fry zucchini in batches in hot oil until just tender; drain well on absorbent paper.

Quarter pepper, remove seeds and membrane. Broil pepper, skin-side-up, until skin blisters and blackens. Peel away skin, cut pepper into thin strips. Slice tomatoes into 8 x ½ inch slices.

Spread all eggplant slices thickly with pesto. Place 4 of the largest eggplant slices on plates, top with zucchini slices, half the tomato slices, another 4 medium eggplant slices, pepper strips, remaining tomato slices then remaining eggplant slices. Drizzle with dressing, cover, refrigerate 2 hours. Decorate with extra pepper strips, if desired.

Pesto: Blend or process basil, garlic, nuts and oil until smooth; stir in cheese.
Dressing: Combine all ingredients in screw-top jar; shake well.
Serves 4.

VEGETABLE NESTS WITH MUSTARD DRESSING

1 leek
1 large carrot
2 large zucchini
4 teaspoons fresh lemon thyme leaves

MUSTARD DRESSING
1 tablespoon butter
2 teaspoons mustard seeds
½ cup dry white wine
½ cup heavy cream
2 teaspoons seeded mustard

Cut leek into ¾ inch x 9½ inch strips. Using a vegetable peeler, peel strips lengthways from carrot and zucchini. Add vegetable strips to pan of boiling water, bring to boil; drain immediately, rinse under cold water, drain on absorbent paper. Take 2 strips of each vegetable, twist into a nest, place on plate. Repeat with remaining vegetable strips. Sprinkle nests with thyme; drizzle with warm mustard dressing.

Mustard Dressing: Heat butter in pan, add seeds, cook, covered, until seeds pop. Add wine, cream and mustard, simmer, uncovered, until thickened slightly.

Serves 4 to 6.

ORIENTAL CUCUMBER SALAD

3 small green cucumbers, thinly sliced
coarse (kosher) salt
2 small fresh red chili peppers,
finely chopped
¼ cup rice vinegar
4 teaspoons Oriental sesame oil
4 teaspoons olive oil
4 teaspoons light soy sauce
2 teaspoons sugar
3 tablespoons mirin
2 teaspoons grated fresh gingerroot

Sprinkle cucumbers with salt, cover, refrigerate 1 hour. Rinse cucumbers under cold water, pat dry with absorbent paper. Combine cucumbers with remaining ingredients in bowl; mix well. Cover, refrigerate 10 minutes. Drain cucumbers and serve; discard marinade.

Serves 4.

BARBEQUED VEGETABLE SALAD

1 eggplant
3 zucchini
coarse (kosher) salt
10oz pumpkin squash
1 large onion
1 red bell pepper, quartered
olive oil

DRESSING
3 tablespoons fresh lemon juice
½ cup olive oil
¼ teaspoon sugar
2 teaspoons drained green
peppercorns, crushed
4 teaspoons drained small capers
1 clove garlic, minced

Slice eggplant and zucchini lengthways into ¼ inch slices. Sprinkle with salt, stand 30 minutes.

Rinse eggplant and zucchini under cold water, drain on absorbent paper. Cut squash and onion into ¼ inch slices. Cut pepper into ¾ inch strips. Brush vegetables with oil, barbeque on both sides until browned. Combine vegetables on plate, top with dressing.

Dressing: Combine all ingredients in screw-top jar; shake well.

Serves 4 to 6.

LEFT: Clockwise from left: Vegetable Nests with Mustard Dressing, Eggplant, Tomato and Zucchini Stacks, Oriental Cucumber Salad. ABOVE: Barbequed Vegetable Salad.

TURNIP AND FENNEL SALAD

1 white turnip
1 fennel bulb, thinly sliced
3 tablespoons pumpkin seed
    kernels, toasted
¼ cup slivered almonds, toasted

VINAIGRETTE
¼ cup olive oil
3 tablespoons cider vinegar
1 teaspoon seasoned pepper
3 tablespoons chopped fresh parsley

Peel turnip, cut into thin strips. Boil, steam or microwave turnip until just tender; drain, rinse under cold water, drain. Combine turnip, fennel, pumpkin seed kernels and nuts in bowl, add vinaigrette; mix well.
Vinaigrette: Combine all ingredients in screw-top jar; shake well.
Serves 4.

BELOW: From top: Turnip and Fennel Salad, Marinated Bocconcini and Tomato Salad.

MARINATED BOCCONCINI AND TOMATO SALAD

Bocconcini best marinated a day ahead; store, covered, in refrigerator.

¼ cup olive oil
2 teaspoons chopped fresh mint
3 tablespoons firmly packed fresh
    basil leaves
2 teaspoons fresh lemon juice
2 teaspoons balsamic vinegar
4 (about 3oz) bocconcini
2 large tomatoes, sliced

DRESSING
¾ cup olive oil
2 teaspoons chopped fresh mint
¼ cup firmly packed fresh basil leaves
½ teaspoon grated lemon zest
1 tablespoon fresh lemon juice

Blend or process oil, herbs, juice and vinegar until smooth. Combine basil mixture and bocconcini in bowl, cover, refrigerate overnight. Remove bocconcini from marinade, discard marinade, cut bocconcini into ¼ inch slices. Serve bocconcini with tomatoes; top with dressing.
Dressing: Blend or process all ingredients until smooth.
Serves 4.

ZUCCHINI, CUCUMBER AND FENNEL SALAD

2 small green cucumbers,
    peeled, seeded
4 zucchini
1 grapefruit
2 tablespoons (¼ stick) butter
2 teaspoons fennel seeds
½ teaspoon sugar
2 teaspoons chopped fresh thyme
4 teaspoons fresh grapefruit juice
4 teaspoons white wine vinegar
2 teaspoons olive oil

Cut cucumbers and zucchini into matchsticks. Using a vegetable peeler, cut peel thinly from grapefruit, avoiding any white pith; cut peel into thin strips.

Heat butter in pan, add zucchini, peel and seeds, cook, stirring, until zucchini are just tender. Strain butter from zucchini mixture; reserve butter. Combine zucchini mixture and cucumber in bowl.

Heat reserved butter in pan, add remaining ingredients, simmer, uncovered, until reduced by half. Top zucchini mixture with butter mixture.

Serves 4.

MIXED VEGETABLE SALAD WITH YOGURT DRESSING

2 stalks celery, chopped
2 tomatoes, chopped
½ cup cooked green peas
6 radishes, chopped
1 red bell pepper, chopped
2 small green cucumbers, seeded, chopped

YOGURT DRESSING
1 teaspoon ground cumin
1 teaspoon ground fennel
½ teaspoon seasoned pepper
1 cup plain yogurt

Combine all ingredients in bowl; add yogurt dressing, mix well.
Yogurt Dressing: Add spices to dry pan, stir over heat until fragrant. Combine spice mixture with yogurt in bowl; whisk until smooth.
Serves 6.

CELERIAC AND CARROT SALAD WITH CAPERS

1 (about 1¼lb) celeriac (celery root)
3 tablespoons white wine vinegar
3 cups water
2 carrots
7oz sliced cooked ham
3 tablespoons drained capers

DRESSING
¼ cup sour cream
⅓ cup mayonnaise
4 teaspoons grated lemon zest
3 tablespoons fresh lemon juice

Peel and cut celeriac into thin strips, place in bowl, cover with combined vinegar and water. Cut carrots and ham into thin strips. Drain celeriac; dry on absorbent paper. Combine celeriac, carrots, ham and capers in bowl, add dressing; mix well.
Dressing: Combine all ingredients in bowl; whisk well.
Serves 6.

WARM CAULIFLOWER WITH CHILI GARLIC DRESSING

1½lb cauliflower, chopped
½ cup sunflower seed kernels
3 tablespoons chopped fresh chives

CHILI GARLIC DRESSING
½ cup olive oil
1 tablespoon sweet chili sauce
3 tablespoons red wine vinegar
3 cloves garlic, minced

Boil, steam or microwave cauliflower until just tender; drain, rinse under cold water, drain. Combine cauliflower, seeds and chives in bowl, add chili garlic dressing; mix lightly. Serve warm or cold.
Chili Garlic Dressing: Combine all ingredients in screw-top jar; shake well.
Serves 4.

ABOVE: From top: Warm Cauliflower with Chili Garlic Dressing, Zucchini, Cucumber and Fennel Salad.
RIGHT: From left: Celeriac and Carrot Salad with Capers, Mixed Vegetable Salad with Yogurt Dressing.

BASKETS WITH VEGETABLES AND GINGERROOT

2 sheets phyllo pastry
oil for deep-frying
1½oz piece fresh gingerroot
1½oz green beans, sliced
2½oz snow peas
2½oz sugar snap peas
2 green onions
½ cup unsalted roasted cashews
1½oz snow pea sprouts

LEMON GINGERROOT DRESSING
1 teaspoon grated fresh gingerroot
2 cloves garlic, minced
3 tablespoons fresh lemon juice
½ teaspoon Oriental sesame oil
½ teaspoon fish sauce
3 tablespoons salad oil
¼ teaspoon light soy sauce

Cut both sheets of pastry in half cross-ways, cut each half into 4. Layer 4 pieces of pastry over inside of lightly oiled double strainer. Press top of strainer onto pastry. Lower strainer into hot oil, holding handles firmly together, deep-fry until pastry is lightly browned; drain basket on absorbent paper. Repeat with remaining pastry.

Peel and slice gingerroot lengthways, cut each slice into thin strips. Deep-fry gingerroot in batches in hot oil until lightly browned; drain on absorbent paper.

Boil, steam or microwave beans and both peas until just tender; drain, rinse under cold water, drain. Cut onions into 2½ inch lengths. Combine beans, peas, onions, nuts and sprouts in bowl. Fill baskets with vegetable mixture, top with lemon gingerroot dressing and fried gingerroot.
Lemon Gingerroot Dressing: Blend or process all ingredients until smooth.

Serves 4.

FRESH BEET AND WATERCRESS SALAD

8 (about 2½lb) fresh beets
3 cups (about 5oz) firmly packed
  watercress sprigs

DRESSING
⅓ cup white wine vinegar
½ cup walnut oil
¼ cup salad oil
1 teaspoon Dijon mustard
2 cloves garlic, minced

Boil, steam or microwave beets until just tender; drain, rinse under cold water, drain. Peel beets, cut into quarters. Combine beets and dressing in bowl, cover, refrigerate 1 hour. Add watercress to beet mixture; mix gently.
Dressing: Combine all ingredients in screw-top jar; shake well.

Serves 4 to 6.

ORANGE AND GREEN VEGETABLE SALAD

¼lb fresh asparagus spears, chopped
7oz broccoli, chopped
5oz snow peas
5oz sugar snap peas
1 small green cucumber, seeded, sliced
1 orange, segmented
4 teaspoons chopped roasted
  hazelnuts

DRESSING
⅓ cup salad oil
4 teaspoons hazelnut oil
3 tablespoons red wine vinegar
4 teaspoons fresh orange juice
½ teaspoon seeded mustard
½ teaspoon sugar

Boil, steam or microwave asparagus, broccoli and both peas until just tender; drain, rinse under cold water, drain. Combine vegetables, cucumber and dressing in bowl; mix well. Top with orange segments and nuts.
Dressing: Combine all ingredients in screw-top jar; shake well.

Serves 4.

CRUDITES WITH TWO DIPS

½ red bell pepper
½ yellow bell pepper
½ bunch (about 10) radishes
1 bunch (about 12) baby carrots
2oz snow peas
3½oz cherry tomatoes
12 quail eggs, hard-boiled

EGGPLANT DIP
2 small eggplants
4 teaspoons olive oil
2 cloves garlic, minced
4 teaspoons fresh lemon juice
3 tablespoons olive oil, extra

¼ teaspoon sambal oelek
3 tablespoons chopped fresh basil
4 teaspoons chopped fresh mint

CARROT DIP
2 large carrots, chopped
1 cup water
1 vegetable bouillon cube
1 clove garlic, minced
¼ teaspoon ground cumin
¼ teaspoon ground coriander
2 teaspoons sherry vinegar
3 tablespoons olive oil

Cut peppers into thin strips. Serve peppers, radishes, carrots, peas, tomatoes and eggs with eggplant and carrot dips.
Eggplant Dip: Halve eggplants lengthways, make diagonal cuts on cut side, place on baking sheet, brush with oil. Bake, uncovered, in 350°F oven about 1¼ hours or until very tender; cool. Scoop out flesh, discard skin. Blend or process eggplants, garlic, juice, extra oil and sambal oelek until smooth, stir in herbs.
Carrot Dip: Combine carrots, water and crumbled bouillon cube in pan, simmer, covered, until carrots are very tender; drain. Process carrots with remaining ingredients until smooth.

Serves 4.

LEFT: Clockwise from back: Orange and Green Vegetable Salad, Fresh Beet and Watercress Salad, Baskets with Vegetables and Gingerroot.
BELOW: Crudites with Two Dips.

MUSHROOM AND ARTICHOKE SALAD

12 drained artichoke hearts
½ teaspoon coriander seeds, crushed
½ teaspoon cuminseed
½lb button mushrooms, quartered
½ cup mung bean sprouts
4 teaspoons chopped fresh parsley
4 teaspoons chopped fresh chives

DRESSING
⅓ cup virgin olive oil
3 tablespoons raspberry vinegar
½ teaspoon sugar

Cut artichokes in half. Combine seeds in dry pan, cook, stirring, until fragrant; cool. Combine artichokes, seed mixture, mushrooms, sprouts, herbs and dressing in bowl; mix well.
Dressing: Combine all ingredients in screw-top jar; shake well.

Serves 4.

GRATED PUMPKIN SQUASH AND ZUCCHINI SALAD

2 zucchini, grated
10oz pumpkin squash, grated
3 tablespoons sesame seeds, toasted

DRESSING
¼ cup mayonnaise
4 teaspoons water
1 teaspoon honey
1½ teaspoons grated fresh gingerroot

CHEESY CROUTONS
1 long bread roll
3 tablespoons butter, melted
⅓ cup finely grated Parmesan cheese
½ teaspoon paprika

Combine zucchini, squash and seeds in bowl, add dressing; mix lightly. Serve with cheesy croutons.
Dressing: Combine all ingredients in screw-top jar; shake well.
Cheesy Croutons: Thinly slice roll diagonally to form croutons. Brush both sides of croutons with butter, place on baking sheet. Bake in 350°F oven about 15 minutes or until lightly browned. Toss croutons in combined cheese and paprika. Place croutons on baking sheet, sprinkle with any remaining cheese mixture, bake further 2 minutes; cool.

Serves 4.

ROASTED BELL PEPPER SALAD

2 red bell peppers
2 yellow bell peppers
2 green bell peppers
4 anchovy fillets, thinly sliced
¼ cup pine nuts, toasted
16 baby black olives

DRESSING
4 teaspoons balsamic vinegar
2 cloves garlic, minced
¼ cup olive oil
4 teaspoons chopped fresh oregano

Quarter peppers, remove seeds and membranes. Broil peppers, skin-side-up, until skin blisters and blackens. Peel away skin. Arrange peppers and anchovies on plate, drizzle with dressing, sprinkle with nuts and olives.
Dressing: Combine all ingredients in screw-top jar; shake well.
Serves 4 to 6.

HERBED CORN SALAD

15oz can baby corn, drained
17oz can whole-kernel corn, drained
2 green onions, chopped

DRESSING
¼ cup salad oil
4 teaspoons cider vinegar
2 teaspoons chopped fresh chives
2 teaspoons chopped fresh basil
1 teaspoon chopped fresh thyme
¼ teaspoon sugar

Cut baby corn into ¾ inch lengths. Combine all corn, onions and dressing in bowl; mix well.
Dressing: Combine all ingredients in screw-top jar: shake well.
Serves 4.

LEFT: From left: Mushroom and Artichoke Salad, Grated Pumpkin Squash and Zucchini Salad.
BELOW: From left: Herbed Corn Salad, Roasted Bell Pepper Salad.

GAZPACHO SALAD

2 small green cucumbers, chopped
4 green onions, chopped
4 tomatoes, chopped
2 red bell peppers, chopped

DRESSING
1 green onion, chopped
¼ cup vegetable juice
3 tablespoons olive oil
4 teaspoons red wine vinegar
½ teaspoon sugar

Combine all ingredients in bowl; mix well, stir in dressing.
Dressing: Combine all ingredients in screw-top jar; shake well.

Serves 6 to 8.

BAKED VEGETABLES WITH CARDAMOM SYRUP

2 large parsnips
1¼lb sweet potato
4 teaspoons light olive oil

CARDAMOM SYRUP
1 lime
4 teaspoons fresh lime juice
¼ cup sugar
¼ cup water
¼ cup white wine vinegar
½ teaspoon cardamom seeds
½ small fresh red chili pepper, finely chopped
2 cloves garlic, thinly sliced
4 teaspoons red currant jelly

Peel and cut parsnips and potato into 1¼ inch pieces. Place parsnips and potato into roasting pan, drizzle with oil. Bake, uncovered, in 375°F oven about 25 minutes or until vegetables are tender, stirring occasionally; cool. Top parsnips and sweet potato with cardamom syrup.
Cardamom Syrup: Using a vegetable peeler, cut peel thinly from lime, avoiding any white pith; cut peel into thin strips. Combine peel with remaining ingredients in pan, stir over heat, without boiling, until sugar is dissolved and jelly melted, then simmer, uncovered, 2 minutes; cool.

Serves 4.

BEET CABBAGE SALAD

1 teaspoon caraway seeds
1¾lb canned baby beets, drained
¼ cabbage, shredded

DRESSING
3 tablespoons cider vinegar
1 teaspoon Dijon mustard
1 teaspoon grated orange zest
1 teaspoon honey
½ cup olive oil

Add seeds to skillet, stir over heat until fragrant. Cut beets into strips, combine with cabbage and dressing in bowl; add seeds.
Dressing: Combine all ingredients in screw-top jar; shake well.

Serves 6.

MARINATED LEEKS

4 leeks
4 teaspoons chopped fresh chives

DRESSING
1 clove garlic, minced
½ cup olive oil
¼ cup balsamic vinegar
4 teaspoons Dijon mustard
1 green onion, finely chopped
1 teaspoon seasoned pepper

Using only white parts of leeks, cut leeks lengthways into quarters. Steam or microwave leeks until tender; drain, pat dry with absorbent paper. Pour dressing over warm leeks; cover, stand at room temperature 2 hours. Serve marinated leeks sprinkled with chives.
Dressing: Combine all ingredients in screw-top jar; shake well.

Serves 4 to 6.

MINTED RED CABBAGE AND ORANGE SALAD

½lb sugar snap peas
½ small red cabbage, shredded
2 large oranges, segmented

MINTY ORANGE DRESSING
½ cup fresh orange juice
4 teaspoons chopped fresh mint
4 teaspoons white wine vinegar
¼ cup salad oil

Boil, steam or microwave peas until just tender; drain, rinse under cold water, drain well. Combine peas, cabbage and oranges in bowl, add minty orange dressing; mix lightly.
Minty Orange Dressing: Combine all ingredients in screw-top jar; shake well.

Serves 4 to 6.

LEFT: Clockwise from left: Beet Cabbage Salad, Baked Vegetables with Cardamom Syrup, Gazpacho Salad.
ABOVE: From top: Marinated Leeks, Minted Red Cabbage and Orange Salad.

WINTER VEGETABLES WITH GARLIC MAYONNAISE

1 carrot
1 parsnip
1 leek
5oz sweet potato
½lb Jerusalem artichokes
15oz celeriac (celery root)
¼ cup fresh lemon juice
4 baby new potatoes
¼ cup dry white wine
¼ cup olive oil
4 teaspoons chopped fresh thyme
4 teaspoons chopped fresh rosemary

GARLIC MAYONNAISE
1 egg
1 egg yolk
½ teaspoon French mustard
4 teaspoons fresh lemon juice
2 cloves garlic, minced
1 cup olive oil
4 teaspoons chopped fresh chives

Cut carrot, parsnip, leek, potato, artichokes and celeriac lengthways into wedges. Add celeriac and juice to pan of boiling water, simmer until tender; drain.

Place remaining vegetable wedges and potatoes in ovenproof dish, sprinkle with wine, oil and herbs. Bake, covered, in 375°F oven 40 minutes, remove leeks. Bake, uncovered, further 30 minutes or until vegetables are tender. Return leeks to dish, add celeriac, bake further 5 minutes or until heated through. Serve warm with garlic mayonnaise.

Garlic Mayonnaise: Process egg, yolk, mustard, juice and garlic until smooth, gradually add oil in thin stream while motor is operating, process until smooth, stir in chives.

Serves 4 to 6.

EGGPLANT WAFERS WITH YOGURT DRESSING

2 teaspoons sesame seeds
2 teaspoons sunflower seed kernels
½ teaspoon coriander seeds
1 teaspoon cuminseed
1 large eggplant, thinly sliced
oil for deep-frying

YOGURT DRESSING
¾ cup plain yogurt
1 clove garlic, minced
½ teaspoon sugar
1½ tablespoons water
1½ tablespoons chopped fresh cilantro

Place seeds on baking sheet, toast in 375°F oven about 5 minutes or until fragrant. Deep-fry eggplant in batches in hot oil until lightly browned; drain on absorbent paper. Place eggplant on plate; top with yogurt dressing, sprinkle with toasted seeds.

Yogurt Dressing: Combine all ingredients in bowl; mix well.

Serves 4.

BROCCOLI AND EGG SALAD

1½lb broccoli, chopped
1 small red onion, sliced
6 green onions, chopped
6 hard-boiled eggs, halved

DRESSING
¾ cup mayonnaise
4 teaspoons fresh lime juice
1 teaspoon seeded mustard
½ teaspoon French mustard

Boil, steam or microwave broccoli until just tender; drain, rinse under cold water, drain. Combine broccoli, onion and green onions in bowl, add dressing; mix gently. Top with eggs.
Dressing: Combine all ingredients in bowl; mix well.

Serves 4 to 6.

CRUNCHY PEA AND NUT SALAD

1lb frozen green peas
4 stalks celery, chopped
1 cup (5oz) unsalted roasted peanuts
⅔ cup macadamias, toasted
8oz can water chestnuts,
    drained, chopped

DRESSING
¾ cup creme fraiche
4 teaspoons light soy sauce
2 teaspoons Oriental sesame oil
¼ teaspoon honey
1 teaspoon fresh lime juice
4 teaspoons chopped fresh parsley

Boil, steam or microwave peas until tender; drain, rinse under cold water, drain well. Combine peas, celery, nuts and water chestnuts in bowl, add dressing; mix well.
Dressing: Combine all ingredients in bowl; mix well.

Serves 6.

LEFT: From left: Eggplant Wafers with Yogurt Dressing, Winter Vegetables with Garlic Mayonnaise.
BELOW: From left: Broccoli and Egg Salad, Crunchy Pea and Nut Salad.

RED BELL PEPPER, ONION AND TOMATO SALAD

2 red bell peppers
1 red onion, sliced
3 tomatoes, sliced

DRESSING
½ cup olive oil
3 tablespoons red wine vinegar
1 clove garlic, minced
4 teaspoons chopped fresh basil
4 teaspoons chopped fresh chives
½ teaspoon sugar

Quarter peppers, remove seeds and membranes. Broil peppers, skin-side-up, until skin blisters and blackens. Peel away skin, cut peppers into ½ inch strips. Combine peppers, onion and tomatoes in bowl, add dressing; mix well. Cover, refrigerate 2 hours.

Dressing: Combine all ingredients in screw-top jar; shake well.

Serves 4 to 6.

BELOW: Clockwise from left: Parsley, Mint and Crisp Bread Salad, Cucumber and Asparagus Salad with Chili Peppers, Red Bell Pepper, Onion and Tomato Salad. RIGHT: From left: Broccoli, Corn and Bok Choy Salad, Potato Salad with Sun-Dried Tomatoes.

CUCUMBER AND ASPARAGUS SALAD WITH CHILI PEPPERS

1lb fresh asparagus spears
4 small green cucumbers, seeded
4 teaspoons light olive oil
2 cloves garlic, minced
4 teaspoons chopped fresh lemon grass
1/4 cup water
2 teaspoons drained green
   peppercorns, crushed
2 teaspoons fish sauce
2 small fresh red chili peppers, sliced
1/4 cup fresh lime juice
1/2 teaspoon sugar

Cut asparagus in half lengthways, then into 2½ inch lengths. Cut cucumbers into 2½ inch thin strips. Heat oil in skillet, add asparagus, garlic and lemon grass, cook, stirring, until fragrant. Add water, peppercorns, sauce, chili peppers, juice and sugar, simmer, covered, about 2 minutes or until asparagus is just tender. Add cucumbers, stir until heated through.

Serves 4.

PARSLEY, MINT AND CRISP BREAD SALAD

2 large pita bread rounds
3 tablespoons olive oil
1 teaspoon dried basil leaves
2 cups firmly packed flat-leafed
   parsley, chopped
1 cup firmly packed fresh mint
   leaves, chopped
4 green onions, chopped
3 tomatoes, chopped
1 small green cucumber,
   seeded, chopped

DRESSING
2 cloves garlic, minced
1/4 cup fresh lemon juice
1/2 cup olive oil
1 teaspoon sugar

Split bread in half; brush split side of bread with oil, sprinkle with basil. Place bread rounds, split side up, on baking sheet, bake in 375°F oven about 5 minutes or until bread is browned and crisp; cool. Break bread into small pieces.

Combine bread, parsley, mint, onions, tomatoes and cucumber in bowl, add dressing; mix well.

Dressing: Combine all ingredients in screw-top jar; shake well.

Serves 6.

BROCCOLI, CORN AND BOK CHOY SALAD

7oz broccoli, chopped
1 bunch (about 3/4lb) bok choy
1 cup (2½oz) bean sprouts
1 red bell pepper, thinly sliced
15oz can baby corn, drained
4 green onions, sliced
1/4 cup chopped fresh cilantro

DRESSING
1/4 cup salad oil
3 tablespoons light soy sauce
1/2 teaspoon Oriental sesame oil
4 teaspoons grated fresh gingerroot
4 teaspoons fresh lemon juice
1 clove garlic, minced

Add broccoli to pan of boiling water, boil, uncovered, until just tender. Add bok choy to pan, return to boil, boil, uncovered, until bok choy is just softened; drain, rinse under cold water, drain. Combine broccoli and bok choy with remaining ingredients in bowl, add dressing; mix well.

Dressing: Combine all ingredients in screw-top jar; shake well.

Serves 4 to 6.

POTATO SALAD WITH SUN-DRIED TOMATOES

2½oz sliced pepperoni
2½lb baby new potatoes, halved
2/3 cup drained sun-dried
   tomatoes, sliced
3 tablespoons pine nuts, toasted

BASIL MAYONNAISE
3 egg yolks
2 cloves garlic, minced
3 tablespoons fresh lemon juice
3/4 cup salad oil
1/2 cup firmly packed shredded
   fresh basil

Cut pepperoni into thin strips. Boil, steam or microwave potatoes until tender; drain; cool. Combine pepperoni, potatoes, tomatoes and basil mayonnaise in bowl; mix well, sprinkle with nuts.

Basil Mayonnaise: Beat egg yolks, garlic and juice in bowl until smooth. Gradually beat in oil a drop at a time, beating constantly, until a little over a quarter of the oil is added. Pour in remaining oil in a thin stream, beating constantly; stir in basil.

Serves 6.

ASPARAGUS AND MUSTARD CRESS SALAD

½lb fresh asparagus spears
1 bunch (about 15) baby carrots
1 red leaf lettuce
½lb mustard cress

MUSTARD DRESSING
4 teaspoons seeded mustard
1 teaspoon Dijon mustard
¼ cup olive oil
3 tablespoons fresh lime juice
½ teaspoon chopped fresh rosemary

Cut asparagus into 3 inch lengths. Trim tops from carrots. Boil, steam or microwave asparagus and carrots until just tender; drain, rinse under cold water, drain. Combine asparagus, carrots, torn lettuce leaves and cress in bowl, add mustard dressing; mix gently.
Mustard Dressing: Combine all ingredients in screw-top jar; shake well.

Serves 4 to 6.

NUTTY BEAN SPROUTS WITH RED BELL PEPPER

1 small iceberg lettuce
3 cups (about ½lb) mung
    bean sprouts
1 red bell pepper, sliced
⅔ cup unsalted roasted cashews
4 teaspoons sesame seeds, toasted

DRESSING
3 tablespoons light soy sauce
3 tablespoons fresh lemon juice
½ cup salad oil
½ teaspoon sambal oelek
1 teaspoon grated fresh gingerroot
1 clove garlic, minced
½ teaspoon Oriental sesame oil

Combine torn lettuce leaves with remaining ingredients in bowl; top with dressing.
Dressing: Combine all ingredients in screw-top jar; shake well.

Serves 6.

WARM PANCETTA AND BELGIAN ENDIVE SALAD

5oz pancetta
6 Belgian endives
3 tablespoons olive oil
1 red onion, sliced
3 tablespoons chopped fresh parsley

Cut pancetta into ¾ inch strips. Cut endives crossways into ¾ inch lengths. Heat oil in pan, add pancetta and onion, cook, stirring, until onion is soft. Add endive, cook, stirring, until endive is just wilted. Add parsley, serve immediately.

Serves 6.

PINK SALAD LEAVES WITH RASPBERRY DRESSING

4 large beet leaves
1 radicchio lettuce
1 red oak leaf lettuce
8 radishes, sliced
1 red onion, halved, sliced

RASPBERRY DRESSING
3 tablespoons raspberry vinegar
⅓ cup salad oil
¼ cup olive oil

Combine torn beet and lettuce leaves, radishes and onion in bowl; drizzle with raspberry dressing.
Raspberry Dressing: Combine all ingredients in screw-top jar; shake well.

Serves 6.

ARUGULA, BASIL AND ONION SALAD

2 bunches (about ½lb) arugula
½ small red onion, thinly sliced
1 cup firmly packed fresh purple
    basil leaves

DRESSING
3 tablespoons sherry vinegar
½ cup olive oil
2 teaspoons horseradish cream
1 teaspoon sugar

Combine arugula, onion and basil in bowl; drizzle with dressing.
Dressing: Combine all ingredients in screw-top jar; shake well.

Serves 4.

LEFT: From left: Nutty Bean Sprouts with Red Bell Pepper, Asparagus and Mustard Cress Salad.
RIGHT: Clockwise from front: Pink Salad Leaves with Raspberry Dressing, Warm Pancetta and Belgian Endive Salad, Arugula, Basil and Onion Salad.

TOMATO PARSLEY SALAD ON OLIVE CROUTES

4 thick slices rye bread
3 tablespoons olive oil
2 teaspoons olive paste
**2 cups firmly packed fresh
    parsley sprigs**
oil for deep-frying
2 tomatoes, sliced
5oz mozzarella cheese, sliced
1½oz snow pea sprouts

DRESSING
¼ cup olive oil
4 teaspoons sherry vinegar
1 clove garlic, minced

Place bread on baking sheet, brush with combined oil and paste. Toast in 350°F oven until crisp. Deep-fry parsley in batches in hot oil until dark green and crisp; drain on absorbent paper. Top croutes with tomatoes, cheese, sprouts and parsley; drizzle with dressing.
Dressing: Combine all ingredients in screw-top jar; shake well.

Serves 4.

ABOVE: From left: Bitter Leaf Salad with Curry Yogurt Dressing, Peachy Leaf Salad with Dill Dressing.
LEFT: Tomato Parsley Salad on Olive Croutes.
RIGHT: Mixed Leaf and Flower Salad.

BITTER LEAF SALAD WITH CURRY YOGURT DRESSING

2 Belgian endives
1 bunch sorrel
2 radicchio lettuce
1 bunch chicory

CURRY YOGURT DRESSING
½ cup plain yogurt
½ teaspoon curry powder
1 teaspoon honey
3 tablespoons cream
4 teaspoons water

Cut large endive leaves in half. Slice sorrel into thin strips. Combine endive, torn lettuce and chicory leaves in bowl; pour curry yogurt dressing over salad, sprinkle with sorrel.
Curry Yogurt Dressing: Combine all ingredients in bowl; mix well.

Serves 6.

PEACHY LEAF SALAD WITH DILL DRESSING

1 bunch (about ¼lb) arugula
2 radicchio lettuce
1¾ cups (about 2oz) watercress sprouts
½lb snow peas
2 peaches, sliced

DILL DRESSING
1 peach, peeled, chopped
⅓ cup plain yogurt
4 teaspoons sour cream
1 teaspoon honey
4 teaspoons chopped fresh dill

Combine arugula, torn lettuce leaves, sprouts and peas in bowl, top with peaches and dill dressing.
Dill Dressing: Blend or process peach until smooth. Add remaining ingredients; blend until combined.

Serves 4 to 6.

MIXED LEAF AND FLOWER SALAD

We used unsprayed edible flower petals such as marigold, viola, strawberry blossom, lavender and nasturtium.

7oz mixed baby salad leaves
¾ cup flower petals

DRESSING
4 teaspoons chopped fresh tarragon
2 tablespoons champagne vinegar
½ teaspoon Dijon mustard
⅓ cup macadamia oil
3 tablespoons olive oil

Combine leaves, petals and dressing in bowl; mix gently.
Dressing: Combine all ingredients in screw-top jar; shake well.

Serves 4.

BEST CAESAR SALAD

6 slices bread
oil for shallow-frying
1 romaine lettuce
½ x 2oz can anchovy fillets, drained, thinly sliced
1 cup (2½oz) grated or flaked Parmesan cheese

DRESSING
1 egg
1 clove garlic, minced
3 tablespoons fresh lemon juice
½ teaspoon Dijon mustard
½ x 2oz can anchovy fillets, drained
¾ cup olive oil

Remove crusts from bread, cut bread into ½ inch cubes. Shallow-fry cubes in hot oil until browned and crisp; drain on absorbent paper. Combine torn lettuce leaves, half the croutons, half the anchovies and half the cheese in bowl, add half the dressing; mix well. Sprinkle with remaining croutons, anchovies and cheese; top with remaining dressing.
Dressing: Blend or process egg, garlic, juice, mustard and anchovies until smooth, pour in oil in thin stream while motor is operating, blend until thick.
Serves 4.

ARUGULA, WATERCRESS AND PEAR SALAD

2 bunches (about ½lb) arugula
2 cups (about 3½oz) firmly packed watercress sprigs
⅓ cup chopped walnuts or pecans
1 large pear, sliced

DRESSING
3 canned pear halves
2 teaspoons red wine vinegar
¼ cup walnut oil

Combine arugula, watercress, nuts and pear in bowl; drizzle with dressing.
Dressing: Drain pears, reserve ⅓ cup syrup. Blend or process pears, reserved syrup, vinegar and oil until smooth; strain.
Serves 6.

BELOW: From left: Best Caesar Salad, Arugula, Watercress and Pear Salad.
RIGHT: Clockwise from top: Chicory and Daikon Salad with Red Bell Pepper Oil, Warm Spinach and Bell Pepper Salad, Radicchio, Fennel and Feta Salad.

CHICORY AND DAIKON SALAD WITH RED BELL PEPPER OIL

1 (about 10oz) daikon
½ bunch chicory
1 small radicchio lettuce

RED BELL PEPPER OIL
4 large red bell peppers
½ cup olive oil

Peel and cut daikon into very thin matchsticks. Combine daikon, chicory and torn lettuce leaves in bowl; drizzle with red bell pepper oil.
Red Bell Pepper Oil: Remove seeds and membranes from peppers. Process peppers until well minced, push through fine strainer into pan; discard pulp. Simmer pepper juice, uncovered, until reduced to ⅓ cup. Combine pepper juice and oil in bowl; mix well.
Serves 4 to 6.

RADICCHIO, FENNEL AND FETA SALAD

1 stalk celery
½ fennel bulb, thinly sliced
1 radicchio lettuce
¼ cup small black olives
¼ cup pimiento-stuffed green olives
2½oz feta cheese, crumbled

DRESSING
⅓ cup extra virgin olive oil
¼ cup fresh lemon juice
1 teaspoon fennel seeds, crushed
2 cloves garlic, thinly sliced

Reserve celery leaves, thinly slice celery. Combine celery leaves, celery, fennel, torn lettuce leaves and olives in bowl; sprinkle with cheese, top with dressing.
Dressing: Combine all ingredients in screw-top jar; shake well.
Serves 4.

WARM SPINACH AND BELL PEPPER SALAD

1 yellow bell pepper
1 red bell pepper
1 bunch (about 1¼lb) spinach
1 small onion, sliced
½ cup olive oil
1 clove garlic, minced
½ teaspoon seasoned pepper
⅓ cup balsamic vinegar

Quarter peppers, remove seeds and membranes. Broil peppers, skin-side-up, until skin blisters and blackens. Peel away skin, cut peppers into strips. Coarsely shred spinach. Combine peppers, spinach and onion in bowl.

Heat oil in skillet, add garlic and seasoned pepper, cook, stirring, 1 minute. Add vinegar, stir until heated through. Add dressing to salad; mix well.
Serves 4.

RED CABBAGE, WATERCRESS AND FETA SALAD

1 romaine lettuce
¼ red cabbage, finely shredded
2 cups (about 3½oz) firmly packed
    watercress leaves
7oz feta cheese, crumbled

DRESSING
1 clove garlic, minced
1 teaspoon chopped fresh thyme
1½ teaspoons Dijon mustard
3 tablespoons red wine vinegar
½ cup olive oil
¼ teaspoon sugar
¼ teaspoon cracked black
    peppercorns
¼ teaspoon paprika

Combine torn lettuce leaves, cabbage and watercress in bowl; sprinkle with cheese, drizzle with dressing.
Dressing: Combine all ingredients in screw-top jar; shake well.

Serves 4 to 6.

BEET CRISP SALAD WITH CITRUS DRESSING

2 zucchini
oil for deep-frying
4 beets, peeled
½ teaspoon celery salt
1 small Boston lettuce
1 small lollo biondo lettuce

CITRUS DRESSING
1 teaspoon grated lime zest
4 teaspoons fresh lime juice
¼ cup fresh orange juice
¼ cup salad oil
1 clove garlic, minced
½ teaspoon sugar

Using vegetable peeler, peel zucchini lengthways to form thin ribbons. Deep-fry zucchini in batches in hot oil until lightly browned and crisp; drain on absorbent paper. Thinly slice beets, deep-fry in batches in hot oil until crisp; drain on absorbent paper. Sprinkle zucchini and beet crisps with celery salt.
    Combine torn lettuce leaves and citrus dressing in bowl, top with zucchini and beet crisps.
Citrus Dressing: Combine all ingredients in screw-top jar; shake well.

Serves 4 to 6.

SPINACH AND THREE SPROUTS SALAD

8 spinach leaves, shredded
4 large Boston lettuce leaves,
    shredded
1 small green cucumber,
    seeded, chopped
8 cherry tomatoes, halved
1 cup (2½oz) mung bean sprouts
1 cup (2½oz) lentil sprouts
1 cup (1½oz) alfalfa sprouts

DRESSING
¼ cup tomato juice
4 teaspoons white wine vinegar
½ teaspoon sambal oelek
1 clove garlic, minced
¼ cup olive oil

Combine all ingredients in bowl, add dressing; mix well.
Dressing: Combine all ingredients in screw-top jar; shake well.
Serves 6.

SPINACH AND MACADAMIA SALAD

1 bunch (about 1¼lb) spinach
1½oz snow pea sprouts
¾ cup macadamias, halved, toasted
½ cup sliced dried apricots

DRESSING
⅓ cup macadamia oil
4 teaspoons white wine vinegar
1 clove garlic, minced
¼ teaspoon sugar

Tear spinach into pieces. Combine all ingredients in bowl, add dressing; mix well.
Dressing: Combine all ingredients in screw-top jar; shake well.
Serves 6.

CHICORY, GOATS' CHEESE AND POMEGRANATE SALAD

1 pomegranate
1 small bunch chicory
1 small green oak leaf lettuce
5oz goats' cheese, crumbled
3 tablespoons chopped fresh chives
3 tablespoons shredded fresh basil

DRESSING
3 tablespoons sherry vinegar
1 clove garlic, minced
½ cup olive oil
¼ teaspoon cracked black
    peppercorns

Remove seeds from pomegranate, discard skin and pith. Combine chicory and torn lettuce leaves in bowl, sprinkle with pomegranate seeds, cheese and herbs; drizzle with dressing.
Dressing: Combine all ingredients in screw-top jar; shake well.

Serves 4 to 6.

LEFT: Clockwise from back: Spinach and Three Sprouts Salad, Red Cabbage, Watercress and Feta Salad, Beet Crisp Salad with Citrus Dressing.
ABOVE: From left: Spinach and Macadamia Salad, Chicory, Goats' Cheese and Pomegranate Salad.

111

ORANGE, ONION AND OLIVE SALAD

2 tablespoons olive oil
2 large onions, sliced
1½ teaspoons grated orange zest
3 tablespoons sugar
3 tablespoons white wine vinegar
⅓ cup fresh orange juice
1 cup (about 1½oz) firmly packed watercress sprigs
3 oranges, segmented
1 green onion, finely chopped
3 tablespoons small black olives
1 tablespoon brown vinegar
4 teaspoons olive oil, extra

Heat oil in skillet, add onions and zest, cook, covered, stirring occasionally, about 10 minutes or until onions are soft. Add sugar, white wine vinegar and juice, simmer, uncovered, about 30 minutes or until thick; cool.

Combine onion mixture and watercress in bowl, top with oranges, green onion and olives. Drizzle with combined brown vinegar and extra oil.

Serves 4.

SPICED TROPICAL FRUIT SALAD

1 coconut
1 papaya, chopped
1 large mango, chopped
1 stalk celery, finely chopped

SPICY COCONUT DRESSING
4 teaspoons chopped fresh chives
1 small fresh red chili pepper, sliced
3 tablespoons chopped fresh cilantro
⅔ cup canned unsweetened coconut milk
3 tablespoons fresh lime juice
1 tablespoon fish sauce
2 teaspoons grated fresh gingerroot
⅛ teaspoon ground saffron

Pierce holes in top end of coconut to extract liquid, discard liquid. Break open coconut, prise off outer shell, break flesh into pieces.

Combine papaya, mango and celery in bowl; top with spicy coconut dressing. Serve with coconut.
Spicy Coconut Dressing: Combine all ingredients in bowl; mix until smooth.
Serves 4 to 6.

LEFT: From top: Spiced Tropical Fruit Salad, Apple and Date Salad, Orange, Onion and Olive Salad.
RIGHT: From top: Grapefruit and Spinach Salad, Fruity Spaghetti Salad.

APPLE AND DATE SALAD

2 red apples
1/2 cup pitted dates
1/4 cup flaked coconut, toasted

DRESSING
1/4 cup dry white wine
1/4 cup salad oil
1/4 cup heavy cream
4 teaspoons fresh lemon juice
2 teaspoons sugar
2 teaspoons honey
2 teaspoons dark rum

Cut apples into thin wedges. Cut dates into thin strips. Combine apples, dates, coconut and dressing in bowl; mix gently.
Dressing: Combine all ingredients in screw-top jar; shake well.

Serves 6.

FRUITY SPAGHETTI SALAD

1 small cantaloupe
1 small pineapple
1/4lb thin spaghetti pasta
1/2lb jarlsberg cheese, cubed
1 cup (5oz) natural whole almonds

MARINADE
4 teaspoons grated lime zest
1/3 cup fresh lime juice
2 teaspoons honey
4 teaspoons grated fresh gingerroot
1 teaspoon sugar

Cut cantaloupe and pineapple into 3/4 inch pieces. Combine fruit and marinade in bowl, cover, refrigerate 1 hour.
Add pasta to large pan of boiling water, boil, uncovered, until just tender; drain, rinse under cold water, drain. Combine undrained fruit mixture, pasta, cheese and nuts in bowl; mix well.
Marinade: Combine all ingredients in bowl; mix well.

Serves 4 to 6.

GRAPEFRUIT AND SPINACH SALAD

1/2 bunch (about 10oz) spinach
2 grapefruit, segmented
1/4 cup Parmesan cheese flakes

DRESSING
3 tablespoons balsamic vinegar
2 teaspoons honey
1/3 cup olive oil
1/2 teaspoon seasoned pepper
1 clove garlic, minced

Top torn spinach leaves with grapefruit and cheese; drizzle with dressing.
Dressing: Combine all ingredients in screw-top jar; shake well.

Serves 4.

FIG AND GRAPE SALAD WITH PROSCIUTTO

4 slices prosciutto
2 bunches (about ½lb) arugula
4 large figs, quartered
3½oz white grapes
3½oz black grapes
2oz blue cheese

DRESSING
4 teaspoons sherry vinegar
3 tablespoons olive oil

Slice prosciutto into thin strips. Place arugula leaves on plate, top with figs, grapes, prosciutto and crumbled cheese; drizzle with dressing.
Dressing: Combine vinegar and oil in screw-top jar; shake well.

Serves 4.

BELOW: From top: Fig and Grape Salad with Prosciutto, Avocado, Asparagus and Strawberry Salad.

AVOCADO, ASPARAGUS AND STRAWBERRY SALAD

½lb fresh asparagus spears, chopped
1 red oak leaf lettuce
1 avocado, sliced
4 teaspoons pistachios

STRAWBERRY DRESSING
¼lb strawberries, chopped
4 teaspoons fresh orange juice
3 tablespoons salad oil
1 teaspoon balsamic vinegar
¼ teaspoon freshly ground black pepper
½ teaspoon sugar

Boil, steam or microwave asparagus until just tender; drain, rinse under cold water, drain. Combine asparagus, torn lettuce leaves and avocado on plate; drizzle with strawberry dressing, sprinkle with nuts.
Strawberry Dressing: Blend or process strawberries and juice until smooth; strain. Combine strawberry puree with remaining ingredients in screw-top jar; shake well.
Serves 4.

PEAR AND APPLE SALAD WITH ROASTED CASHEWS

4 Asian pears, sliced
1 red apple, sliced
2 stalks celery, chopped
½ cup golden raisins
½ cup unsalted roasted cashews

DRESSING
4 egg yolks
2 cloves garlic, minced
3 tablespoons fresh lemon juice
¼ cup macadamia oil
½ cup salad oil
3 tablespoons sour cream
2 teaspoons honey
2 teaspoons milk

Combine pears, apple, celery, raisins and dressing in bowl; mix well. Serve sprinkled with nuts.
Dressing: Blend or process egg yolks, garlic and juice until smooth. Gradually add oils in a thin stream while motor is operating, blend until thickened. Stir in cream, honey and milk; mix well.

Serves 6.

CANTALOUPE AND BLUEBERRY SALAD

1 tablespoon butter
½ teaspoon curry powder
1 teaspoon grated fresh gingerroot
½ cup chopped macadamias
1 stalk celery, sliced
2 green onions, sliced
1½lb cantaloupe, sliced
3½oz fresh blueberries
¼ cup loosely packed
   watercress sprigs

DRESSING
⅓ cup whipping cream
2 tablespoons milk
4 teaspoons fresh lemon juice
4 teaspoons chopped fresh parsley
½ teaspoon seeded mustard

Heat butter in skillet, add curry powder, gingerroot and nuts, cook, stirring, until nuts are coated in curry mixture and lightly browned; cool. Combine nut mixture, celery, onions, cantaloupe and blueberries in bowl; drizzle with dressing and top with watercress.
Dressing: Combine all ingredients in bowl; mix well.
Serves 4.

GREEN PAPAYA SALAD

10 (about 2oz) long beans
1 green papaya
⅓ cup unsalted roasted peanuts
3 tablespoons dried shrimp
1 clove garlic, minced
1 small fresh green chili pepper,
   finely chopped
4 teaspoons palm sugar
3 tablespoons fresh lime juice
1 teaspoon fish sauce
2 teaspoons chopped fresh cilantro

Cut beans into 1½ inch lengths. Boil, steam or microwave beans until just tender; drain, rinse under cold water, drain. Peel and coarsely grate papaya. Blend or process peanuts, shrimp, garlic, chili, sugar, juice and sauce until well combined. Combine beans, papaya and shrimp mixture in bowl; mix well, sprinkle with cilantro.
Serves 4.

BELOW: From top: Green Papaya Salad, Cantaloupe and Blueberry Salad.

PINEAPPLE, GRAPES AND BROCCOLI WITH CHEESE DIP

1 large pineapple
7oz broccoli, chopped
7oz black grapes

CHEESE DIP
½ cup cottage cheese
¼ cup plain yogurt
4 teaspoons fresh orange juice
4 teaspoons chopped fresh chives

Cut pineapple in half, remove and discard core. Cut into ¼ inch slices. Boil, steam or microwave broccoli until tender; drain, rinse under cold water, drain.
   Serve pineapple, broccoli and grapes with cheese dip.
Cheese Dip: Combine all ingredients in bowl; mix well.
Serves 4.

ABOVE: From back: Pineapple, Grapes and Broccoli with Cheese Dip, Pear and Apple Salad with Roasted Cashews.

BASIC SALADS & DRESSINGS

Prepared with care, the familiar, tried and true salads are always winners. Our favorite recipes featured here are quick to make, using readily available ingredients. They all serve 10 so there's plenty for entertaining at barbeques, buffets or banquets. However, if you're serving fewer people, the quantities can easily be adjusted without spoiling the flavor. It's also helpful to have a variety of basic dressings at your fingertips, ready to suit a variety of dishes and all tastes. Most dressings can be made a day ahead, but the salads are best made just before serving.

PASTA SALAD

1lb pasta twists
3 tablespoons olive oil
7oz button mushrooms, sliced
3 stalks celery, chopped
1 large red bell pepper, chopped
1 large green bell pepper, chopped
17oz can whole-kernel corn, drained
3 tablespoons chopped fresh parsley
1 cup bottled Caesar salad dressing

Add pasta to pan of boiling water, boil, uncovered, until just tender; drain, rinse under cold water, drain. Combine pasta with remaining ingredients; mix well.

Serves 10.

GREEN SALAD

1½ iceberg lettuce
1 red leaf lettuce
2 stalks celery, chopped
1 green bell pepper, sliced
2 small green cucumbers, sliced
4 green onions, chopped
1 avocado, sliced

DRESSING
3 tablespoons fresh lemon juice
1 clove garlic, minced
⅛ teaspoon sugar
½ teaspoon French mustard
½ cup olive oil

Combine torn lettuce leaves with remaining ingredients in bowl, add dressing; mix well.
Dressing: Combine all ingredients in screw-top jar; shake well.

Serves 10.

TOMATO AND ONION SALAD

7 tomatoes, sliced
2 onions, sliced
⅔ cup shredded fresh basil
1 cup bottled Italian dressing

Combine tomatoes and onions in bowl; sprinkle with basil, top with dressing.

Serves 10.

COLESLAW

½ cabbage, shredded
2 carrots, grated
1 red bell pepper, finely chopped
4 green onions, finely chopped
1 cup bottled coleslaw dressing

Combine all ingredients in bowl; mix well.

Serves 10.

LEFT: Clockwise from left: Pasta Salad, Green Salad, Tomato and Onion Salad.
ABOVE RIGHT: Clockwise from left: Rice Salad, Coleslaw, Bean Salad.

RICE SALAD

2 cups (14oz) long-grain rice
17oz can whole-kernel corn, drained
15¼oz can pineapple chunks in natural juice, drained
1 red bell pepper, chopped
1 green bell pepper, chopped
1 cup (¼lb) cooked green peas
4 green onions, chopped
½ cup chopped fresh parsley
⅔ cup bottled Italian dressing

Add rice to large pan of boiling water, boil, uncovered, until just tender; drain, rinse under cold water, drain. Combine rice with remaining ingredients in bowl; mix well.

Serves 10.

BEAN SALAD

8oz canned corn, lima beans and peppers
8¾oz can red kidney beans
2 x 15oz cans three bean mix
2 x 8oz cans garbanzo beans
2 stalks celery, finely chopped
4 green onions, finely chopped
⅓ cup chopped fresh parsley
¼ cup chopped fresh mint
⅔ cup bottled French dressing

Rinse and drain canned corn mixture and beans, combine with remaining ingredients in bowl; mix well.

Serves 10.

POTATO SALAD

4lb baby new potatoes, halved

DRESSING
1 cup bottled mayonnaise
½ cup bottled Italian dressing
½ cup sour cream
6 green onions, chopped
¼ cup chopped fresh chives
2 teaspoons French mustard
2 teaspoons sugar

Boil, steam or microwave potatoes until tender; drain, rinse under cold water, drain. Place potatoes in bowl, add dressing; mix well.
Dressing: Place all ingredients in bowl, whisk until combined.
Serves 10.

BEET SALAD

5 x 16oz cans sliced beets, drained
1¼ cups sour cream
3 tablespoons prepared horseradish
¼ cup chopped fresh chives
4 teaspoons water

Rinse beets under cold water; drain well. Cut into ¼ inch strips. Combine sour cream, horseradish, chives and water in bowl, add beets; mix lightly to combine.
Serves 10.

BELOW: From back: Beet Salad, Potato Salad.

MAYONNAISE

Here is our basic recipe for mayonnaise and 5 simple variations; each recipe makes about 1 cup.

BASIC MAYONNAISE

2 egg yolks
4 teaspoons fresh lemon juice
½ teaspoon dry mustard
½ cup olive oil
½ cup salad oil
3 tablespoons milk, approximately

Blend or process egg yolks, juice and mustard until smooth. Add combined oils gradually in thin stream while motor is operating; blend until thick. Spoon mayonnaise into bowl; whisk in enough milk to give desired consistency.

CURRIED MAYONNAISE

4 teaspoons curry powder

Add curry powder to dry pan, stir over heat until fragrant; cool. Blend curry powder with egg yolks, follow method for basic mayonnaise recipe.

HERB MAYONNAISE

3 tablespoons chopped fresh chives
3 tablespoons chopped fresh parsley
3 tablespoons chopped fresh basil

Follow method for basic mayonnaise; whisk herbs into completed mayonnaise.

LIME MAYONNAISE

2 teaspoons grated lime zest
4 teaspoons lime juice, approximately

Omit milk from basic recipe, whisk zest into completed mayonnaise, whisk in enough juice to give desired consistency and taste.

THOUSAND ISLAND MAYONNAISE

1/3 cup tomato paste
1/3 cup tomato ketchup
4 teaspoons Worcestershire sauce
1/2 teaspoon tabasco sauce

Omit milk from basic recipe, whisk paste and sauces into completed mayonnaise.

GARLIC MAYONNAISE

3 cloves garlic, minced

Blend or process garlic with egg yolks, follow method for basic mayonnaise.

ABOVE: Top row from left: Basic Mayonnaise, Lime Mayonnaise, Thousand Island Mayonnaise. Second row from left: Herb Mayonnaise, Curried Mayonnaise, Garlic Mayonnaise.

SALAD DRESSINGS

Here are 3 simple dressings to add zest and variety to salads. Each recipe makes about 1 cup.

FRENCH DRESSING

¼ cup white vinegar
¾ cup salad oil
½ teaspoon sugar
1 teaspoon French mustard

Combine all ingredients in screw-top jar; shake well.

ITALIAN DRESSING

3 tablespoons white wine vinegar
3 tablespoons fresh lemon juice
½ teaspoon sugar
2 cloves garlic, minced
¾ cup olive oil
4 teaspoons chopped fresh basil
4 teaspoons chopped fresh oregano

Combine all ingredients in screw-top jar; shake well.

NUTTY DRESSING

¼ cup fresh lemon juice
4 teaspoons white wine vinegar
⅓ cup salad oil
⅔ cup walnut or hazelnut oil

Combine all ingredients in screw-top jar; shake well.

ABOVE: From left: French Dressing, Italian Dressing, Nutty Dressing.

GLOSSARY

Here are some terms, names and alternatives to help

everyone understand and use our recipes perfectly.

ALCOHOL: is optional, but gives a particular flavor. Use fruit juice or water instead, if preferred, to make up the liquid content required.

ARTICHOKE HEARTS: available from supermarkets and delicatessens in bottles, cans and bulk.

ARUGULA: a green salad leaf; pictured on page 124.

BACON SLICES: we used thick slices.

BEANS AND PEAS, DRIED: adzuki, black-eyed peas (also known as black-eyed beans), borlotti, broad (fava), garbanzo, red kidney, black (turtle) - see below.

BLACK BEAN SAUCE: made from fermented whole and crushed soy beans, water and wheat flour.

BLACK BEANS, SALTED: fermented, soy beans. Canned and dried black beans can be substituted. Drain and rinse canned variety. Leftover beans will keep for months in airtight container in the refrigerator. Mash beans when cooking to release flavor. Used in Asian recipes.

BOK CHOY: Chinese chard. Use leaves and young, tender parts of stems.

BOUILLON POWDER, INSTANT: 1 cup broth is the equivalent of 1 cup water plus 1 crumbled bouillon cube (or 1 teaspoon bouillon powder). If you prefer to make your own fresh broth see recipes on page 123.

BULGUR: also known as cracked wheat, is wheat which has been cracked by boiling, then redried; mostly used in Middle Eastern cooking.

BUTTER: use salted or unsalted butter.

CAPERS: pickled buds of a Mediterranean shrub used as flavoring.

CELERIAC: tuberous root with brown skin, white flesh and a celery-like flavor; see below.

ABOVE: Celeriac.

CHICORY: a salad leaf, also known as curly endive; pictured on page 124.

CILANTRO: also known as Chinese parsley and coriander, it is essential to many South-East Asian cuisines. A strongly flavored herb, use it sparingly until accustomed to the unique flavor.

CINNAMON STICK: dried inner bark of the shoots of the cinnamon tree.

COCONUT

Canned Unsweetened Cream and Milk: available from supermarkets and Asian food stores.

Flaked: flaked coconut flesh.

Shredded: thin strips of dried coconut.

ABOVE: Clockwise from top: broad beans, red beans, black (turtle) beans, garbanzo beans, red kidney beans, black-eyed peas. Center: adzuki beans.

COUSCOUS: a fine cereal made from semolina.

CREAM FRAICHE: a mixture of sour cream with fresh cream; available from supermarkets and specialty food stores.

CSABAI: a type of Hungarian salami, available from most delicatessens.

CURRY POWDER: a convenient combination of powdered spices. It consists of chili, coriander, cumin, fennel, fenugreek and turmeric in varying proportions.

DAIKON: a basic food in Japan, it is also called giant white radish.

DRIED SHRIMP: dried salted baby shrimp available from Asian food stores.

FENNEL: has a slight aniseed taste when fresh, ground or in seed form. Fennel seeds are a component of curry powder.

FENNEL BULB: is eaten uncooked in salads or may be braised, steamed or stir-fried in savory dishes.

FISH SAUCE: made from the liquid drained from salted, fermented anchovies. Has a strong smell and taste; use sparingly.

FIVE-SPICE POWDER: a pungent mixture of ground spices which includes cinnamon, cloves, fennel, star anise and Szechuan peppers.

FLOUR

Self-Rising: substitute all-purpose flour and double-acting baking powder in the proportions of 1 cup all-purpose flour to 2 level teaspoons of double-acting baking powder. Sift together several times before using.

GARAM MARSALA: often used in Indian cooking, this spice combines cardamom, cinnamon, cloves, coriander, cumin and nutmeg in varying proportions. Sometimes pepper is used to make a hot variation.

GHEE: a pure butter fat available in cans and cartons, it can be heated to high temperatures without burning because of the lack of salts and milk solids.

GINGERROOT

Fresh or green: scrape away outside skin and grate, chop or slice as required. To preserve fresh, peeled gingerroot, cover with dry sherry in a jar and refrigerate. It will keep for months.

GREEN ONIONS: also known as scallions.

GREEN PEPPERCORNS: available in cans or jars, pickled or in brine.

HARISSA: sauce or paste made from dried red chilies, garlic, oil and, sometimes, caraway seeds.

HOISIN SAUCE: a thick sweet Chinese barbeque sauce made from a mixture of salted black beans, onion and garlic.

HUMMUS: a paste of garbanzo beans, tahini, garlic, lemon juice and olive oil.

JERUSALEM ARTICHOKE: a root vegetable resembling knobbly potatoes or gingerroot; see below.

ABOVE: Jerusalem artichokes.

JUNIPER BERRIES: dried berries of an evergreen tree; they are the main ingredient in gin.

KONBU: kelp seaweed used in Japanese cooking as an ingredient in dashi, to flavor rice for sushi, and as a relish.

LAMB PROSCIUTTO: uncooked, unsmoked, cured lamb; ready to eat when bought.

LEMON GRASS: available from Asian food stores; needs to be bruised or chopped before using.

LENTILS: dried pulses. There are many different varieties, usually identified and named after their color.

LETTUCE: more unusual varieties include Boston, romaine, lollo rosso, lollo biondo, radicchio, green oak leaf and red oak leaf; some are pictured on page 124.

LONG BEANS: long thin beans used in Asian cooking, available from Asian food stores.

MAFALDE PASTA: ripple edged strips of pasta.

MIRIN: sweet rice wine used in Japanese cooking.

MIXED SPICE: blend of ground cinnamon, allspice and nutmeg.

MIZUNA: a green salad leaf; pictured on page 124.

NORI: a type of dried seaweed used in Japanese cooking as a flavoring,

garnish or for sushi. Sold in thin sheets.

OIL: we used olive oil, light olive oil and salad oil where specified.

Olive: virgin oil is obtained only from the pulp of high-grade fruit. Pure olive oil is pressed from the pulp and kernels of second-grade olives. Extra virgin olive oil is the purest quality virgin oil.

OKRA: a green, ridged, immature seed pod, also called lady's fingers; see below.

ABOVE: Okra.

ORIENTAL SESAME OIL: made from roasted, crushed white sesame seeds; used as a flavoring.

OYSTER-FLAVORED SAUCE: a rich brown sauce made from oysters cooked in salt and soy sauce, then thickened with starches.

PALM SUGAR: very fine sugar from the coconut palm. It is sold in cakes, also known as gula jawa, gula melaka and jaggery. Palm sugar can be substituted with brown or black sugar.

PAPPADAMS: made from lentils and sold in packages in different sizes.

PARSLEY, FLAT-LEAFED: also known as Italian parsley or continental parsley.

PASTRAMI: highly seasoned smoked beef ready to eat when bought.

PHYLLO PASTRY: tissue-thin pastry bought chilled or frozen.

PICKLED PINK GINGERROOT: vinegared gingerroot in paper-thin shavings.

POMEGRANATE: a dark red colored tropical fruit with small seeds encased in juicy red pulp.

PROSCIUTTO: uncooked, unsmoked cured ham; ready to eat when bought.

PRUNES: whole dried plums.

PUMPKIN SEED KERNELS: dried hulled pumpkin squash seeds.

PUMPKIN SQUASH: we used several varieties; any type can be substituted for the other.

RICE VERMICELLI: rice noodles.

SAFFRON: available in strands or ground form. The quality varies.

SAMBAL OELEK (also ulek or olek): a paste made from chilies and salt.

SEA SCALLOPS: we used sea scallops with orange coral (roe) attached.

SEASONED PEPPER: a combination of black pepper, sugar and bell pepper.

SEMOLINA: the hard part of wheat which is sifted out and used mainly for making pasta.

SESAME SEEDS: there are 2 types, black and white; we used the white variety in this book.

SNOW PEAS: also known as Chinese pea pods.

SORREL: has broad, oval-shaped leaves with a bitter, slightly sour taste; pictured on page 124.

SOY SAUCE: made from fermented soy beans. The light sauce is generally used with white meat, and the darker variety with red meat. There is a multi-purpose salt-reduced sauce available, also Japanese soy sauce.

SPINACH: a soft-leafed vegetable, delicate in taste. Young Swiss chard leaves can be substituted for spinach.

STAR ANISE: the dried star-shaped fruit of an evergreen tree. It is used sparingly in Chinese cooking and has an aniseed flavor.

SUGAR: we used coarse granulated table sugar, unless otherwise specified.

SUGAR SNAP PEAS: small pods with small, formed peas inside; they are eaten whole, cooked or uncooked.

SUNFLOWER SEED KERNELS: dried husked sunflower seeds.

SWEET POTATO: we used an orange-colored sweet potato unless otherwise specified.

TABASCO SAUCE: made with vinegar, hot red chilli peppers and salt; use sauce sparingly.

TAHINI (SESAME PASTE): made from crushed sesame seeds.

TERIYAKI SAUCE: based on the lighter Japanese soy sauce; contains sugar, spices and vinegar.

TOFU: made from boiled, crushed soy beans. We used firm tofu in this book. Buy it as fresh as possible; keep any leftover tofu in the refrigerator under water, which must be changed daily.

TOMATO

Ketchup: we used tomato ketchup.

Paste: a concentrated tomato puree used as a flavoring.

Sun-Dried Tomatoes: dried tomatoes, sometimes bottled in oil.

VEGETABLE JUICE: we used V8 vegetable juice available in cans and cartons.

WASABI PASTE: green horseradish.

WATERCRESS: has small, deep green, rounded leaves with a peppery flavor; pictured on page 124.

WINE: we used good-quality dry white and red wines.

YEAST: allow 2 teaspoons (1/4oz) active dry yeast to each 1/2oz of fresh yeast if substituting one for the other.

MAKE YOUR OWN BROTH

BEEF BROTH
4lb meaty beef bones
2 onions
2 stalks celery, chopped
2 carrots, chopped
3 bay leaves
2 teaspoons black peppercorns
20 cups water
12 cups water, extra

Place bones and unpeeled chopped onions in roasting pan. Bake, uncovered, in 400°F oven about 1 hour or until bones and onions are well browned. Transfer bones and onions to large pan, add celery, carrots, bay leaves, peppercorns and water, simmer, uncovered, 3 hours. Add extra water, simmer, uncovered, further 1 hour; strain.

Makes about 10 cups.
- ■ Broth can be made 4 days ahead.
- ■ Storage: Covered, in refrigerator.
- ■ Freeze: Suitable.
- ■ Microwave: Not suitable.

CHICKEN BROTH
4lb chicken bones
2 onions, chopped
2 stalks celery, chopped
2 carrots, chopped
3 bay leaves
2 teaspoons black peppercorns
20 cups water

Combine all ingredients in large pan, simmer, uncovered, 2 hours; strain.

Makes about 10 cups.
- ■ Broth can be made 4 days ahead.
- ■ Storage: Covered, in refrigerator.
- ■ Freeze: Suitable.
- ■ Microwave: Not suitable.

FISH BROTH
3lb fish bones
12 cups water
1 onion, chopped
2 stalks celery, chopped
2 bay leaves
1 teaspoon black peppercorns

Combine all ingredients in large pan, simmer, uncovered, 20 minutes; strain.

Makes about 10 cups.
- ■ Broth can be made 4 days ahead.
- ■ Storage: Covered, in refrigerator.
- ■ Freeze: Suitable.
- ■ Microwave: Not suitable.

VEGETABLE BROTH
1 large carrot, chopped
1 large parsnip, chopped
2 onions, chopped
6 stalks celery, chopped
4 bay leaves
2 teaspoons black peppercorns
12 cups water

Combine all ingredients in large pan, simmer, uncovered, 1 1/2 hours; strain.

Makes about 5 cups.
- ■ Broth can be made 4 days ahead.
- ■ Storage: Covered, in refrigerator.
- ■ Freeze: Suitable.
- ■ Microwave: Not suitable.

SORREL

BOSTON LETTUCE

MIZUNA

CHICORY

LOLLO ROSSO LETTUCE

WATERCRESS

ARUGULA

RADICCHIO LETTUCE

RED OAK LEAF LETTUCE

ROMAINE LETTUCE

GREEN OAK LEAF LETTUCE

BELGIAN ENDIVE

INDEX

CUP & SPOON MEASURES

To ensure accuracy in your recipes use standard measuring equipment.

a) 8 fluid oz cup for measuring liquids.
b) a graduated set of four cups – measuring 1 cup, half, third and quarter cup – for items such as flour, sugar, etc.
When measuring in these fractional cups level off at the brim.
c) a graduated set of five spoons: tablespoon (½ fluid oz liquid capacity), teaspoon, half, quarter and eighth teaspoons.
All spoon measurements are level.

We have used large eggs with an average weight of 2oz each in all our recipes.

Salads

Sensational recipes for all occasions

COUNTRY COOKING

Healthy Heart Cookbook

VEGETARIAN COOKING

THE BEST SEAFOOD RECIPES

Italian COOKING CLASS COOKBOOK

CHICKEN COOKBOOK

PLUS duck, quail, turkey, goose and more

PASTA COOKBOOK

More than 170 recipes

CHINESE COOKING CLASS COOKBOOK

STARTERS AND SOUPS

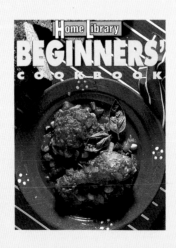

BEGINNERS' COOKBOOK

FINGER FOOD

Best ever party food
Tempting hot and cold savouries
Do ahead and freezing tips